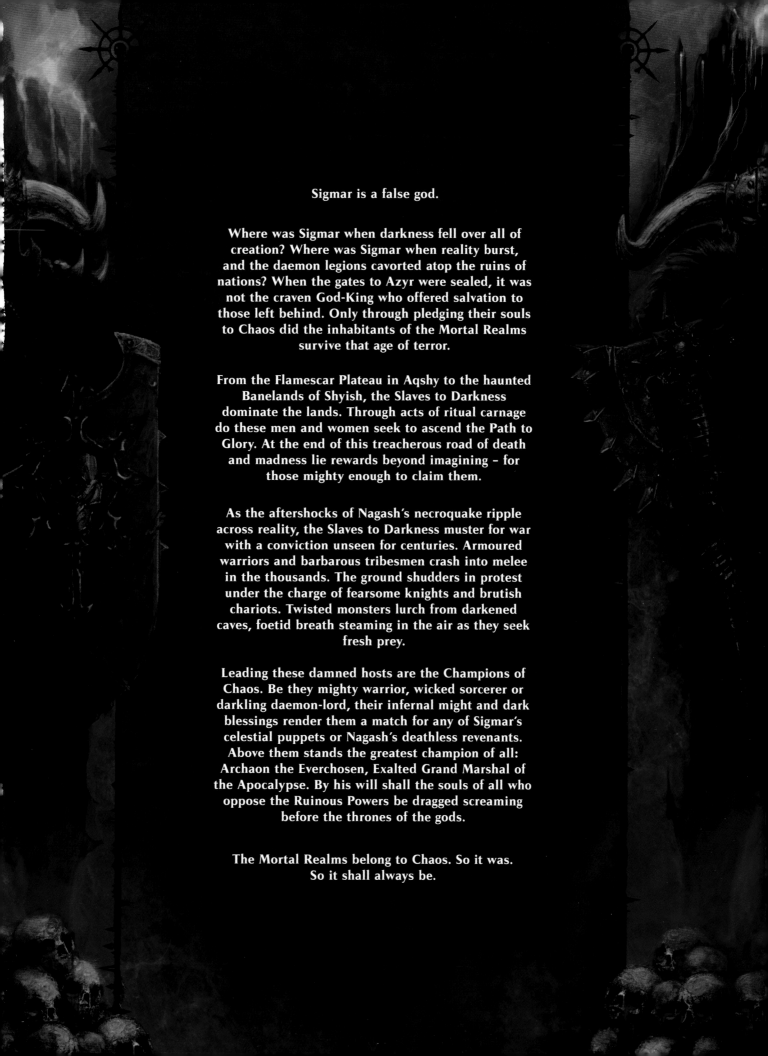

Sigmar is a false god.

Where was Sigmar when darkness fell over all of
creation? Where was Sigmar when reality burst,
and the daemon legions cavorted atop the ruins of
nations? When the gates to Azyr were sealed, it was
not the craven God-King who offered salvation to
those left behind. Only through pledging their souls
to Chaos did the inhabitants of the Mortal Realms
survive that age of terror.

From the Flamescar Plateau in Aqshy to the haunted
Banelands of Shyish, the Slaves to Darkness
dominate the lands. Through acts of ritual carnage
do these men and women seek to ascend the Path to
Glory. At the end of this treacherous road of death
and madness lie rewards beyond imagining – for
those mighty enough to claim them.

As the aftershocks of Nagash's necroquake ripple
across reality, the Slaves to Darkness muster for war
with a conviction unseen for centuries. Armoured
warriors and barbarous tribesmen crash into melee
in the thousands. The ground shudders in protest
under the charge of fearsome knights and brutish
chariots. Twisted monsters lurch from darkened
caves, foetid breath steaming in the air as they seek
fresh prey.

Leading these damned hosts are the Champions of
Chaos. Be they mighty warrior, wicked sorcerer or
darkling daemon-lord, their infernal might and dark
blessings render them a match for any of Sigmar's
celestial puppets or Nagash's deathless revenants.
Above them stands the greatest champion of all:
Archaon the Everchosen, Exalted Grand Marshal of
the Apocalypse. By his will shall the souls of all who
oppose the Ruinous Powers be dragged screaming
before the thrones of the gods.

The Mortal Realms belong to Chaos. So it was.
So it shall always be.

CONTENTS

PRODUCED BY THE WARHAMMER STUDIO
With thanks to The Faithful for their additional playtesting services.

Knight of the Fifth Circle (pg 28), The Many Gifts of Godblade (pg 32), The Weight of Sacrifice (pg 36)
and Echoes of Eternity (pg 44) written by Aaron Dembski-Bowden.

From the back of his dread steed Dorghar, Archaon leads the armies of the Dark Gods to further conquests, the bedrock of the Mortal Realms warping beneath their tread.

THE HORDES OF CHAOS

Where the worshippers of the Dark Gods march, the Mortal Realms tremble. Under the gaze of their dread pantheon, the Slaves to Darkness carve their way through all who stand before them in pursuit of glory. At their head stride some of the most powerful servants of Chaos, forever seeking new challenges and conquests.

Clad in hellish iron and wielding cruel rune-marked blades, the Slaves to Darkness spread war across the Mortal Realms. To look upon them is to witness the doom of civilisation made flesh; barbarous tribes march alongside chosen warriors swollen with the favour of the gods. Their weapons glow with baleful light, while ragged banners bearing twisted sigils snap in the hot air. As the hordes of the damned crash into the enemy, the roars of fell monsters assault the senses, their very presence warping the lands around them into forms of unrecognisable horror.

Yet even these are not the most dreaded warriors of the ruinous hosts. That dark honour belongs to the Champions of Chaos. Brutish chieftains, fallen knights and cunning sorcerers vie to earn the favour of the gods, their lives dedicated to battle and carnage in pursuit of divine favour.

As they slay in the name of the Dark Powers, these champions accrue blessings granted by their godly masters. Their bodies are twisted to better suit the whims of their patron, and the aura of power that surrounds them – not to mention the spreading tales of their glorious slaughters and malevolent exploits – draws fellow worshippers of Chaos from across the lands to join their warbands. The more glory they reap for their god, the more rewards they shall earn, and the larger their conquering hosts will grow.

For all their great power, the majority of Chaos Champions nevertheless meet a grim end. Those who fall in battle are the lucky ones, though their souls are destined to be dragged to the Realm of Chaos and consumed by the thirsting gods. For many, the 'gifts' of the gods prove too much to bear, their minds and bodies sundered by the power of raw Chaos flowing through them.

The fate of these great warlords is to devolve into little more than hideous spawn-things. Yet even this horrific end is not enough to dissuade many aspiring champions from stepping upon the Path to Glory. For a rare few, those who consistently please the gods and possess the strength of will to master their dark blessings, the ultimate reward awaits – immortality as one of the feared Daemon Princes, and an eternity of battle in the name of Chaos.

Death, spawndom or daemonhood – in the end every worshipper of Chaos, from the lowliest Marauder to the mightiest Champion, will meet one of these three fates. There is no act, no matter how heinous or vile, that these damned souls will not commit in pursuit of glory everlasting.

TRIUMPH OF DARKNESS

Were a cartographer foolish enough to venture into the tortured lands beyond Sigmar's nascent cities, they would soon find themselves in the domains of the Slaves to Darkness. Here the scent of death lingers on the wind, and the ground is wracked with tectonic agony. Piles of stacked skulls dot the landscape where the hordes of Chaos have passed. Mutated carrion birds circle in search of fresh prey, while grim monoliths raised in tribute to the Dark Gods intermittently pierce the horizon and radiate a sinister aura.

It is doubtful that such a traveller would ever leave those lands, for the worshippers of the Dark Gods relish meting out brutality upon those they deem trespassers. The weakling servants of the God-King may claim that they are reclaiming their rightful lands, but the Slaves to Darkness see things differently – in their eyes, it is these outsiders and upstarts who are the invaders, and who would contest the rightful domain of the gods.

'What is best in all creation? To crush the weak. To burn their lands to blackened cinder. To catch the gaze of the Powers Beyond. These things, and these things alone.'
- Kardok Varx, Lord of the Thrice-Born Horde

The Slaves to Darkness are the most widespread human inhabitants of the Mortal Realms, particularly in more primal realms such as Aqshy and Ghur. The dead certainly outnumber them, as do the skaven, the grots and the Beasts of Chaos, yet none of these have conquered so vigorously as humanity. In many cases these mortals assemble into barbarous tribes, yet amongst their number are also fallen arcane sects, cursed knightly orders and degenerate cults. It is they, not the children of Sigmar, who typify the masses of humanity found in the Mortal Realms. Across battlefields filled with deathly energies, sorcerous technology and incarnate deities, they fight with sharpened axes and faith in their gods, bartering their souls in return for the power not merely to survive such constant war, but to thrive in it.

The Age of Chaos – during which the Pantheon of Order was broken and the legions of the Dark Gods burst through into reality – brought the Slaves to Darkness into ascendency, but the seeds of damnation were planted long before those bloody centuries. The lost years of the Age of Myth concealed hidden evils beneath their shining veneer. It was the aim of Sigmar and his godly pantheon to create a paradise for their worshippers, and in their arrogance they had dared to hope that the Mortal Realms were a reality unmarred by the taint of Chaos.

Yet the Dark Gods desired the realms greatly, and they knew much of mortal fallibility. The Pantheon of Order had uplifted great swathes of humanity through the arts of civilisation, yet in many cases echoes of ancient tribal ways remained. The worship of older powers lingered on the edge of many cultures' consciousnesses. Gradually, the Dark Gods whispered into the ears of countless peoples, disguising themselves with the faces of these venerable and familiar deities.

Little by little the Chaos Gods corrupted civilisations across the realms. Aqshian plain-dwellers found their martial contests growing bloodier, while in soaring library-cities throughout Hysh scholars and philosophers pursued dangerous forms of lore with the obsessive conviction of true zealots. Perhaps in better days the Pantheon of Order could have detected these signs and worked to stamp out such growing malignancy, yet even the gods had become divided through the machinations of Chaos and their own clashing egos.

When the dam finally broke, the daemonic legions of the Ruinous Powers swept all before them in a hurricane of shocking violence. Landscapes twisted and writhed in the grip of Chaos, and many mortals began to pay homage to the Ruinous Powers simply to survive. Though the God-King and his allies fought valiantly, the disastrous Battle of Burning Skies spelled the end of organised resistance within the realms. Sigmar was forced to retreat to Azyr, and the other gods hid their people away as best they could, or otherwise abandoned them to

survive alone. In their absence, the madness unleashed upon the realms saw more mortals pledge themselves to Chaos in desperation or lust for power.

So have the Slaves to Darkness claimed dominion over much of the Mortal Realms. The lowliest amongst them are not necessarily evil – they are still human, with all the range of emotion and experience that such implies. They love and they hate, they feel joy and despair, and they can find momentary respite in a skin of Aqshian flame-ale or camaraderie with fellow warriors. Yet the gods they worship and the acts performed in their service are fundamentally corrupting. To rise high amongst the Slaves to Darkness is to truck with daemons and sorcerers. It is not only to court fell powers from beyond, but also to bask in their fickle attention.

Even one who seeks to use the power of Chaos for noble causes will eventually find their soul remade as the gods' plaything, for it is the nature of Chaos to despoil and defile even the purest of intentions. Its worshippers are eternally bound to walk a road that leads to nothing but their own demise, or being remade in the image of their god for evermore – and in so doing, losing the essence of who they once were. When the Path to Glory is walked, the price is always the soul. Those who bear the brand of Chaos are, therefore, all slaves of darkness in the truest sense of the word. All, but one.

THE THREE-EYED KING

The hosts of Chaos are fractious and divided, for such is the inherent nature of the Path to Glory. A would-be champion must be willing to go to any length to achieve power and greatness. All, however, owe obedience to Archaon, for he is the Everchosen, the favoured warlord of the Dark Gods, the Exalted Grand Marshal of the Apocalypse. Any who defy his will are trampled into dust by the Varanguard, the infamous Knights of Ruin, cleaved in twain by Archaon's own fearsome daemonblade, or destined for an eternity of torment as a result of being devoured by his colossal three-headed steed, Dorghar.

Even daemon lords must take care in the presence of the Everchosen. Archaon is a veritable demigod of darkness, and by his hand have the armies of Chaos laid waste to the Mortal Realms. Only Azyr still has not yet felt his wrath. Yet the Everchosen is more than just a mighty warrior. Few can match Archaon in the arena of strategy, and for many long years has he plotted how to smash open the gates of the heavens and lay waste to the Celestial Realm. Ancient antipathy exists between Archaon and Sigmar, for the Everchosen has brought death to the God-King's servants since the time of the world-that-was. Only when Azyrheim burns and daemons defile the ruins of Sigmaron will Archaon know satisfaction.

Now, as the Soul Wars rage on, the Slaves to Darkness prepare to undertake their own crusade of reconquest. The tribal conflicts must cease – the gains made by Sigmar and the remnants of his weakling pantheon must be reversed. Across the Mortal Realms new champions arise, eager to attract the gaze of the gods and the Everchosen through their malefic deeds. It is to be an age of opportunity and slaughter beyond even the excesses of the Age of Chaos. The Dark Gods are united in one thing alone – the desire to conquer the Mortal Realms in their entirety – and their worshippers will see the realms burned to cinders before they surrender their hard-won dominion.

Beneath tortured skies and banners marked with the symbols of fell gods, the Slaves to Darkness seek nothing less than to conquer all of creation. Countless mortal tribes and civilisations have pledged themselves to Chaos, and at their head rides Archaon the Everchosen - favoured of all the gods - and his dreaded knights, the Varanguard.

THE PATH TO GLORY

To gain greater power, and ultimately to attain immortality through ascension to daemonhood, is the ambition of all Slaves to Darkness. Yet the road to achieve such an end is always long and bloody, and for many proves lethal. Even should a champion triumph in battle, the gifts of the gods do not always prove beneficial…

To become a Champion of Chaos initially requires nothing more than to pledge one's soul to the dark pantheon. For many inhabitants of the realms every day provides a new form of horror under the boot of their ruinous oppressors. It is no wonder then that a significant number choose to sell their souls to the powers of Chaos and seek to better their lot through conquest. After all, it is preferable to be the victor than the vanquished.

Not all champions are created equal, however. Most are slain before they catch divine attention. Others simply lack the skill to prosper in the war-ravaged realms. Then there are those who, in their devotion or lust for domination, fall deep into the worship of but one of the Dark Gods. Be they frenzied Bloodbound or bloated Rotbringer, these warriors are soon suffused with the power of their chosen deity and swiftly come to embody their will in the Mortal Realms.

Yet whilst these blessed warriors also seek daemonhood, they cannot be said to truly walk the Path to Glory. For although a lord of the Slaves to Darkness will likely find that their personality draws them into the sphere of a certain aspect of Chaos, by rejecting the quickest road to power they attract the interest of the Brothers in Darkness. Gifts and boons are granted unto them as they achieve greater glories, all the better to sway the champion to the exclusive service of one god or another. There are few blessings that the Dark Powers cannot grant, and a god may reward one whose deeds please them even if that champion has already begun to gravitate towards one of that deity's rivals. Though these champions' souls are as forfeit upon

their demise as any other worshipper of Chaos, within them remains a spark of individuality that the Dark Gods loathe and covet in equal measure. Such rapacious beings always lust for that which they do not possess.

Whatever their reasons for stepping upon the Path to Glory, a Champion of Chaos soon becomes addicted to accumulating more and more power. At first, the rewards they receive seem relatively simple; their natural strength will be bolstered, or they may be bequeathed a suit of rune-marked iron forged by the Furnace Kings of Azgorh. Many champions will also begin to revere a particular deity at this point, though even as they channel their chosen god's powers they will still offer prayer and supplication to appease the others.

As time goes by, however, the gifts of the gods will inevitably grow more bizarre; the champion's eyes may pop out on stalks, or perhaps their legs will bend backwards in sickening fashion. They will gain limbs, or lose them. Claws, fangs and tails will sprout across their bodies, as well as stranger appendages taking the form of lashing pseudopods or crowns of flame-wreathed horns. There is no rhyme or reason to these gifts, and for every obviously useful reward the champion receives – a fearsome daemon weapon, greater command of the arcane, or their armour fused to their skin to form an impenetrable hide – they may receive any number of 'boons' that serve no easily discernible purpose.

Complicating matters further is the capricious nature of the Chaos Gods themselves. It is almost impossible to predict what will please these beings, and a champion can be seen to 'lose favour' in a matter of moments. An all-conquering lord can devolve into a hulk of misshapen flesh known as a Chaos Spawn seemingly at random, while one destined for little but violent death is catapulted to glory as the eye of the gods falls upon them.

On occasion, these sudden reversals in status are deliberate. Yet more often than not such devolution or ascension stems from the gods proving too generous with their dubious gifts. These beings do not think in mortal terms, and care little for the effect their 'blessings' have on those who court their favour; more than one champion who has consistently pleased their patron has been overwhelmed by the sheer amount of mutative power uncaringly bestowed upon them.

Despite their fractious nature, one quality unites all successful Champions of Chaos – their unearthly charisma. It is the nature of power to be attracted to power, and those who seek to walk the Path to Glory often begin by following one who has progressed further along that dark road. As a champion rises in the favour of the Ruinous Powers, fellow warriors of the gods will naturally be drawn to their side and form the core of their expanding armies.

These warbands are the fundamental building blocks of almost every grouping of the Slaves to Darkness. They can range from the immediate members of a champion's tribe to many thousands of blade-sworn killers. Warbands constantly grow and shrink in size as warriors break off to form their own conquering hordes, are slain in battle or are joined by new would-be favoured. The greatest lords will have many lesser champions fighting for them, and are able to attract the most powerful servants through the manifest blessings they have earned.

Before achieving daemonhood, a Champion of Chaos must dedicate themselves to one god above all others. Ascension first requires total submission. Those who make such a pledge, and attract the notice of their chosen deity, bear a divine mark upon their flesh – be it an ever-bleeding rune, cluster of pustules, cackling daemon-familiar or even stranger sign. This is no mere brand, for it allows the marked to draw upon a measure of their god's power. Marked champions exude potent auras of divine might, empowering those who share their devotion.

Some Slaves to Darkness do not bear the mark of any god; often these are young warriors who are yet to choose a patron, or hoary veterans who have survived for decades while worshipping the different aspects of their cultural pantheon with equal fervour. Though the gods will inevitably tire of such indecision, these unmarked – who can be said collectively to worship Chaos Undivided, for they do not treat one god with greater primacy than any other – remain deadly foes. Their deeds still earn boons from the gods, who seek to tempt such unclaimed souls into their worship. Yet their command of their own destiny – for the time being – fills these warriors with a great fervour, and compels them to fight with utter fearlessness to forge their own dark legend.

CONQUERORS OF THE REALMS

The infernal dominions of the Slaves to Darkness can be found all across the realms. Countless lands have suffered under their fury, and even with the dawning of the Age of Sigmar and the resurgence of enemies old and new, the vice-like grip held by these warlords and champions of Chaos upon the Mortal Realms remains strong.

The purview of Chaos is not to create, but to corrupt and despoil. Everything that is forged, constructed or otherwise brought into being by the followers of the Dark Gods is suffused with evil. As they wage their wars the Slaves to Darkness remake the very realms themselves in their own baleful image; every land conquered by the tribes soon becomes a physical tribute to their interpretation of the dark pantheon.

The empires of the Slaves to Darkness can be found all across each realmsphere save Azyr, the Realm of Heavens. Some tribes have even ranged towards their home realm's Perimeter Inimical, into the lands where the power of magic resonates most strongly. Few return from these perilous lands, and those who do claim to have heard the voices of the gods themselves. The crusades fought by Sigmar Heldenhammer and the former Pantheon of Order to reclaim their ancestral domains have yet to regain even a tenth of the ground conquered by the Slaves to Darkness. Their outposts and cities are mere beachheads in a sea of unremitting malice, pinpricks of light – though not necessarily purity – flickering within a choking abyss.

Those lands in thrall to the Slaves to Darkness were won through acts of terror and slaughter. These conflicts have not ceased, and centuries of territorial warfare have kept the blades of the tribes sharp. Many champions walk the Path to Glory through such conquests, proving their devotion by raising fell monoliths to the gods upon the bones of their enemies. When the armies of Order, Death or Destruction attempt to carve out new territory for themselves, the Slaves to Darkness stand ready to meet them with hellforged steel and ruinous might – and to embark on new conquests of their own.

STRONGHOLDS OF EVIL

Around every enclave of relative civilisation are great swathes of land still under the iron grip of the Slaves to Darkness. It is not uncommon for multiple warbands, tribes and far-ranging hordes to dwell within these dark domains, though each area will typically be ruled by a single overlord. Many warbands and lesser champions will have sworn themselves to these black-hearted rulers, bound together through a complex, semi-feudal structure defined by the power and favour of each subordinate champion.

The boundaries of these territories are constantly shifting; a champion will only rule while they can prove their worthiness, and all possess rivals they must constantly be on guard against. When the clarion call to war is sounded, however, these ancient enmities are put aside – at least for a time – and armies of the Dark Gods from all across their vast conquered territories will join forces.

Many of the dark tribes are nomadic, wandering wherever the call of the gods takes them. Most tribes do, however, have their own favoured hunting grounds; to solidify their claim over these conquered lands, the overlords of the Slaves to Darkness raise all manner of imposing fortifications from dark metal and blackened bone. These strongholds are known by various names, such as blackspires, dreadholds and monolith-forts. To approach a fortress of the Slaves to Darkness is to court painful death – and worse. The screams of those captured by the Chaos hordes ring endlessly from within, while the armaments mounted upon the angular walls glow with a sinister light, powered by the bound daemons that rage within them.

A TIME-CURSED EMPIRE
The lands west of Steel Spike have been taken in Tzeentch's name.

THE VALRHAF

THE SCALPED

GORETIDE

HALLOWHEART

THE TIMESTOLEN

TEMPEST'S EYE

GOLDENMANE MONUMENT

HAMMERHAND COAST

TRIBES OF THE GREAT PARCH

THE VARANSPIRE

Though many of these strongholds have become the stuff of dark legend, there is one whose infamy eclipses all others. Its name is spoken only in whispers; even the mightiest daemon-kings can be cowed into silence by thought of the torments that lurk behind its spiked crenellations and blood-drenched walls. This is the Varanspire, and it is the fortress of the Everchosen himself.

Rising high at the centre of the Eightpoints – that strange interstitial land that offers passage to the heart of each of the realms – the Varanspire's scale defies comprehension. Within tall towers that pierce the Realm of Chaos itself, Archaon's seers scry the twisting paths of the future, feeding such knowledge to the Everchosen and his inner circle. Within the Varanspire's colossal walls can be found mustering grounds for vast armies alongside every imaginable horror, from writhing nests of twisted flesh to shrines to the Dark Gods that defy all natural laws.

Greatest of these sanctums, located at the Varanspire's black heart, is the Chamber of the Vanquished. Within can be found rows of twisted pillars, ghostly faces writhing in agony across their surface. Ragged banners torn from defeated foes sway in unearthly winds. Dominating the chamber is a throne forged from the ossified souls of kings. It is a throne upon which Archaon has never sat, nor shall he until his conquest of the Mortal Realms is complete. Though several of the arcways – the colossal Realmgates of the Eightpoints, capable of transporting whole armies at once – were torn from the Everchosen's grasp during the Realmgate Wars, still the hordes of Archaon march to battle across the Mortal Realms, the desire for glory and domination burning in the heart of each servant of Chaos.

RAIDERS FROM THE INFERNO
The Candescent Raiders blaze from within. It is said they can charge through Aqshy's infernos without pause.

A WOUND IN REALITY
The Clavis Rift has allowed Khorne's influence to seep in.

THE CLAIM OF LORD ZARONAX

CANDESCENT RAIDERS

ANVILGARD

SCAVENGE KINGS OF ARIDIAN

SUPPLICANTS OF THE WEAL

DOOM LORDS OF AHRAMENTIA

VOSTARGI MONT

COAST OF A THOUSAND EYES

BLADES OF THE BLOOD QUEEN

GORETIDE

TRIBES OF THE BURNING BLOOD

THE ASHEN HORDE

HAMMERHAL AQSHA

VANDIUM

THE CRIMSON HORDE

GORETIDE

ORDER OF THE SINFUL THRONE

FORT DENST

FORT IGNIS

THE BRASS LEGION

THE CHAOS GODS

Impossibly ancient beings who dwell within the roiling nightmare of the Realm of Chaos, the Dark Gods gain their terrible power from the accumulated passions and sins of mortalkind. It is these dread entities to whom the Slaves to Darkness pray before each battle, seeking the strength to slaughter their rivals.

KHORNE, THE BLOOD GOD

Khorne is the Blood God, oldest of all the Chaos powers. He is a being of mindless, absolute violence, who cares not from where the blood flows – only that it does. From atop his throne of skulls, Khorne's raging bellows echo throughout the Realm of Chaos and across the Mortal Realms. Vast armies of mortals and daemons march in his name, bringing the Blood God's creed of everlasting bloodshed to every corner of creation.

Although a tribe may view the god of war as an honourable or even darkly noble figure, in truth Khorne is neither of these things. Dealing brutal and bloody death is the only way to maintain the favour of this furious deity. He takes particular savage joy in witnessing allies turn upon one another, and many of his devoted will readily slaughter one another when no other enemy presents themselves. This said, however, Khorne has no patience for duplicity. He reserves a particular loathing for magic, and views sorcerers as cowards of the foulest breed. No practitioner of the arcane arts has ever been bestowed with Khorne's mark, save Archaon – and this is only due to the unique position the Everchosen holds in the eyes of the dark pantheon.

The Godtouched of Khorne, known as the Bloodmarked, are the most savage of all Slaves to Darkness. Though they have yet to join the chosen ranks of the Bloodbound – either through degenerating into a cannibalistic Bloodreaver, or undergoing the Red Baptism and being remade as a Blood Warrior – their warbands are a terrifying force in battle. Eight is Khorne's sacred number, and thus each Bloodmarked champion will draw eight bands of followers to their side before launching their bloody crusades. As the master of the warband slaughters their enemies, their followers are infused with even greater fury, blades endlessly rising and falling to carve through their enemies with relentless fervour. There is no foe that the Bloodmarked will not eagerly battle against, yet their favourite enemies are the followers of Slaanesh – for Khorne despises the hedonistic Prince of Pleasure above all others, and the mere sight of one bearing the Dark Prince's brand stokes the furnace-hot fury of the Bloodmarked to new heights.

TZEENTCH, ARCHITECT OF FATE

Of all the Chaos Gods, it is Tzeentch who bears the most names: the Architect of Fate, the Great Conspirator and the Lord of Flux are just some of his multifarious titles. From his domain at the heart of the Impossible Fortress he plucks at the strings of causality, manipulating the skeins of destiny to his own unknowable ends. While he may be worshipped in countless guises as a benevolent god of fate and self-improvement, the Architect of Fate considers all mortals little more than pawns in his grand cosmic game. If he chooses to protect some of his champions, it is only because they have another, greater role to play in manipulations yet to come.

Tzeentch is empowered by the hope of mortals, and by the desire to change and better one's station that is present to a degree within all humans. As such, he has a natural rivalry with Nurgle, god of despair and acceptance of the inevitable. This is not to say that Tzeentch can be trusted to make good on his promises of power: his gifts are the most mutagenic and strange of all, and those who catch his gaze regularly end their days either slain by an ambitious rival or as a writhing mass of flesh and tentacles. Those who survive are particularly dangerous foes, however, and the Godtouched of Tzeentch are unlike any other. Each of these Fatesworn was once a figure of some import amongst their tribe, and thus a prime target for the attention of the Great Manipulator, for Tzeentch craves the worship of the powerful and influential first and foremost. Having seen but a sliver of Tzeentch's true face, these warriors have been driven entirely mad, drawn from their old lives into his service. Their warbands are divided into groups of nine warriors, representing their master's particular numerological obsession. Magic clings to the Fatesworn, a gift from the greatest patron of sorcery of all the Chaos Gods, and flickers of arcane power surround them at all times – spiteful flux-incantations drawn from the heart of Tzeentch's realm, and ready to be unleashed upon the foe.

NURGLE, FATHER OF PLAGUES

Wherever sickness blossoms, wherever the tendrils of desperation grip the hearts of mortals, there can be found the touch of Grandfather Nurgle. His spheres are corruption and morbidity, and he takes a foul joy in the spreading of decay. His power is great but cyclical, waxing when sickness stalks the land and waning as his beloved plagues recede. Nurgle's nature is perhaps the most difficult for those not bound to his service to comprehend. Though he is empowered by despair and entropy, the Lord of Corruption is a jolly, gregarious, even loving figure. His daemons and mortal servants are all his children, and from his cauldron at the centre of his rotting manse Nurgle brews new plagues to 'gift' unto the Mortal Realms. Those wracked by these sicknesses then take succour in the Plaguefather's rotting grasp, filled with a morbid vitality even as their bodies become foul and bloated. So does Nurgle propagate a twisted cycle, offering mortals a measure of reprieve from blights that he himself unleashed upon them.

The Plaguetouched of Nurgle seek to grow closer to their foul patron as they plunge deeper into the embrace of decay. The Lord of Corruption has little desire to mislead his faithful, and the many differing depictions of Nurgle found amongst the dark tribes tend to bear the closest resemblance to the true deity out of any of the gods. He is a vile mirror of primitive gods of fertility and the harvest, and like them is surrounded by life – though Nurgle's favoured creatures are flies, maggots and fat-bodied vermin. Most beloved of this rancid god are his mortal champions. Only one who has dedicated themselves to the spread of sickness, so all may wallow in the filth of despair, can hope to truly gain Nurgle's favour and undertake a regenesis as one of the infamous Rotbringers. Though they have yet to rise so high in their lord's esteem, the Plaguetouched warbands – organised into seven groups, for Nurgle has ever held a strange fixation with this number – are bestowed with all manner of bloated blessings, their swollen bodies filled with caustic bile that condemns any it touches to a painful and particularly disgusting death.

SLAANESH, THE DARK PRINCE

Alone of the Dark Gods, Slaanesh is divinely beautiful. Neither male nor female, the Dark Prince is the youngest and most vital of the pantheon – Slaanesh's power comes from no one emotion, but the intensity of all, and any pleasure or anguish felt to excess feeds this hungering being. It is this that makes Slaanesh's worship so tempting to mortals, for many seek only the slightest excuse to discard all code of conduct and lawful bindings and indulge their wildest, most hedonistic desires. It is also this that inspires such uncertainty in Slaanesh's brothers, for while they may hold ascendancy for now, it is possible that Slaanesh may eventually rise to eclipse them all – for whatever emotion or yearning empowers them empowers the Dark Prince also, provided it is felt with a great intensity.

Yet that day may be long in coming, for Slaanesh's throne sits empty, the decadent god imprisoned in a place between shadow and light by the vengeful aelven pantheon. Though the Dark Prince may be bound, however, it is impossible to chain Slaanesh's power entirely. Those champions who satiate their darkest vices in increasingly perverse fashion may find themselves growing more attuned to Slaanesh's truest nature; alone of the Godtouched, these devotees rarely seek to be actively claimed by their patron, but instead naturally fall into the circumstance somewhere along the endless promenade of depravity they walk.

Made up of six warrior-bands, one for each of the Circles of Seduction found within Slaanesh's kingdom, these Pleasurebound warbands are a scourge on all that is pure and decent. A substantial number choose to fight in the Hedonite hosts, either despoiling countless lands alongside the daemons of Slaanesh, relentlessly seeking out the lost god, or even – in the case of the most narcissistic champions – attempting to claim the Lord of Pleasure's vacant throne for themselves. Just as many will remain part of their original tribe however, or journey to attach themselves to new Hordes and particularly sadistic champions, chasing new and increasingly depraved forms of sensation upon the Path to Glory with which to gratify themselves.

THE ENDLESS PANTHEONS

The Slaves to Darkness tribes worship the great powers of Chaos in many different forms and aspects. Would-be champions pray to these beings and seek their blessings as necessity demands, yet it is not uncommon for a tribe to favour a single deity – and in so doing, eternally shackle their souls to one of the Dark Gods.

ASPECTS OF CARNAGE

If one constant can be observed within the Mortal Realms, it is war. Small wonder then that so many human tribes and civilisation pay homage to Khorne, the Blood God. By a thousand names is the deity of slaughter known: the Red Hound, Kharneth, the Axe Father, Arkhar, the Brass Belladonna or the Blood Kraken. There are even some amongst the dark tribes who claim that Khaine, whose name is screamed in devotion by the mysterious aelf-gladiatrixes of Ulgu, is but another reflection of this primal lord of blood.

The sacraments performed to these warlike divinities vary, though most agree that they can only be properly worshipped on the battlefield. Every warrior of the Slaves to Darkness is likely to whisper a prayer to their culture's deity of battle on the eve of conflict – especially those who dwell in the fiery lands of Aqshy, where the 'red gods' are worshipped with particular fervour. Through acts of slaughter, champions attract the gaze of these bloodthirsty patrons; their skin may turn coal-black or arterial red, and their weapons – of which the axe is the most favoured – will radiate an unearthly aura of fury.

The enduring image of a warrior who has been marked by the Lord of Carnage is that of the howling berserker, and in many instances this proves accurate to the point that whole tribes are overcome with frothing fury. Yet these are not the only figures to be receive the mark of the battle-god. Fallen knightly orders will often take an avatar of war as their patron, while in Chamon there are those tribes who worship spirits of mechanised death, and are divinely blessed for each new murderous invention they craft. Despite their differences, however, all these godly figures share an utter loathing of sorcery. The universal Lord of Blood despises those who would employ magic as a crutch for their own weakness, and its devoted warriors will take any excuse to launch brutal witch-purges amongst their neighbouring tribes.

THE MANY FACES OF FATE

Even those who claim not to believe in predestination thank the gods when they pass through an arrow-storm unscathed, or when their blade bites deep into the vulnerable spot of an enemy's armour. Some go further, worshipping the Change God Tzeentch in a variety of forms. Tchar, the Lord of the Shifting Breeze, the Great Eagle, Valedactine; all these beings, and more besides, are honoured by those Slaves to Darkness who seek mastery over the shifting tides of destiny.

The power of fate is worshipped across the realms, and for all manner of reasons. Hunters will beseech it to guide their path towards a bountiful kill, while expectant parents will kneel at scintillating altars and offer prayer or ritual sacrament to ensure a mighty destiny for their offspring. It has been observed by the Slaves to Darkness that those who court the divine aspects of change are inevitably changed themselves upon receiving too much of the power they sought. Yet despite this, or perhaps because of it, the worshippers of the fated path are amongst the most feared servants of Chaos. They tend to possess a revolutionary spirit and a great sense of their own predestined importance. Their actions can seem bizarre, yet each contributes to an overarching whole that carries them one step further along the Path to Glory.

There is no greater cause of change in the cosmos than magic, and so it is unsurprising that many champions have a connection to this mysterious force. Though few are actively wizards, it is not uncommon for these warriors to receive snapshot visions of the future, warning them of incoming danger and allowing them to protect themselves accordingly. The strange arcane aura that surrounds these Slaves to Darkness also voraciously feeds on spells and hexes that come too close, and on occasion magical force hurled against them will be outright dissipated, barely hindering their march towards their destined fate.

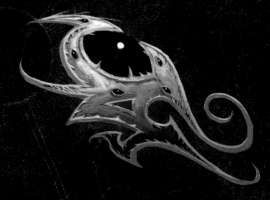

THE COLOURS OF DECAY

Within the Ghyranite kingdom of Erosia can be found tribes of the Slaves to Darkness who worship a kindly goddess known as Mother Mort. Their enemies do not consider her so benevolent, for Mother Mort's gifts take the form of rot, decay, and an inevitable end to all things. Yet to the inhabitants of Erosia there is no shame in this, for it is through devotion to their morbid matron that they have survived in the plague-touched lands. If their bodies are wracked by sickness and their frames grow emaciated through blight, this is considered a small price to pay for the foetid strength to prosper.

This is just one example of the manner in which worship of Nurgle has spread across the Mortal Realms. Onogal, Nielglen, the Rusting Patriarch, the King of All Flies – these are but some of the names by which the primordial cycle of life and death is acknowledged by the Slaves to Darkness. It may seem strange to outsiders that there are those amongst the mortal tribes who would willingly pay homage, and even seek the blessing, of the spirit of decay. Yet in the darkest places of the realms where all hope has long since faded, many believe – not wrongly – that the only way to survive disease and despair is to embrace them. There are even some tribes that worship at the altar of vermin-headed gods of ruin and corruption, cladding themselves in rat-skin cloaks and dancing ecstatically around burning bushels of crops. They are considered outsiders by most Slaves to Darkness, however, and their contempt for even the foulest forms of life sees them particularly hunted by the worshippers of disease.

Those who fall deep into the worship of contagion soon come to bear its mark, for the Chaos power of corruption is renowned for a dark sort of 'generosity' towards its followers. Many champions bestowed with this rancid brand find themselves with a jolly new lease on life, for a disease remains strong and vital even as it kills its host. Their weapons soon become blighted with verdigris and rust, yet never lose their edge – in fact, they only become more dangerous, deadly toxins and potent maladies dripping from their killing edge. Surrounding these pox-marked warriors are swathes of fat-bodied flies that buzz and drone endlessly, obfuscating their advance and constantly reminding these worshippers of foulness that their loving patron is forever watching, and eagerly seeking new initiates for their sickly congregations.

AVATARS OF DEPRAVITY

Though they chase victory in the name of the gods, it is no surprise that most followers of Chaos seek to gratify their own desires along the Path to Glory. Slaanesh eagerly embraces such supplicants, whether they appeal to him directly, or via one of his many guises. For some, the pursuit of these sensations for their own sake becomes an addiction. The spoils of victory and the adulation of their fellow warriors present a lure that is almost irresistible to a considerable number of Slaves to Darkness. Drawn into the grip of self-obsession, many of these champions fall to the worship of pleasure itself.

The depravities performed by those devoted to the worship of sensation – an aspect of Chaos that can take many forms both fair and foul, such as Loesh the Serpent, the Shining Wyrm, the Horned Man or Shornaal of the Gilded Pavilion – are the stuff of legend. Yet not all these beings are patrons of depravity alone. In many cases they are prayed to for success in creative pursuits indulged by the dark tribes. Many metal-shapers or tellers-of-tales have produced works of surprising beauty through entreating their tribe's godly aspect of excess and dedicating their entire soul to their craft.

Curiously, the multifarious deities reflecting the universal Chaotic aspect of excess are often believed to be particularly distant from their servants, and even their brother deities. Many of Loesh's worshippers believe that he lies chained upon the bed of Ghyran's Sea of Elemental Truths, bound there in ages past by the fey inhabitants of the Jade Kingdoms. Amongst the Dreaming Clans of Hysh, it is claimed that the King-Queen of Forbidden Secrets speaks to its supplicants only through mirrors. Some Slaves to Darkness actively seek these absent beings, but most are content that their blessings can still be reaped. Filled with an irrepressible mania, the devotees of pleasure hurtle across the battlefield at a terrifying pace. Even as they carve through the foe these damned warriors display a sinuous grace, delighting in the pain they give and receive. Most depraved of all these libertines are their warleaders, for walking the path of excess inevitably leads to pursuing darker and darker desires. The greatest champions are treated as living deities by their followers, and entire nations of Slaves to Darkness kneel at their feet and seek to satisfy their every unearthly whim.

THE SOUL WARS

Though it spanned many mortal lifetimes, the Age of Chaos did not last forever. As Sigmar's Tempest rolled across the heavens, the Slaves to Darkness were suddenly beset by those they had once crushed – and though they met each of these challenges with grim enthusiasm, worse was still to come.

Though the Age of Chaos represented the triumph of the Slaves to Darkness, it also carried the seeds of disaster for the followers of the gods. The inherent instability of the Ruinous Powers threatened to accomplish what organised resistance could not. In the absence of any worthy foe the worshippers of Chaos were wont to turn on one another to satiate their destructive impulses. On account of their widespread conquests it was the Slaves to Darkness who led much of this internecine conflict; countless warbands clashed, each champion seeking to ascend the Path to Glory over the bones of their slain rivals.

Even as he subjugated hundreds of kingdoms across the realms, from the Howling Cities of Ghur's Beastplains to the aerial empire of Zepheria, always the Everchosen schemed how to bring down the gates of the Celestial Realm. This is not to say that the other realms were spared Archaon's attention. Across the Realm of Beasts his armies fought the brutal Greenskin Wars, while the Battle of Black Skies saw Nagash cast down by the Slayer of Kings – albeit even this could not slay the Lord of Undeath permanently. Yet in the depths of his black heart, Archaon's greatest desire remained always to topple the God-King's throne.

Before Archaon could unleash his armies against Azyr, however, Sigmar counter-attacked. Wreathed in lightning and wielding storm-blessed weapons, the Stormcast Eternals descended to take the fight to the hordes of the Ruinous Powers. The Slaves to Darkness were caught utterly off guard. Their lives had been spent fighting fellow Chaos worshippers or the rampaging tribes and clans of Destruction. Few were the forces of Order that still stood against the hordes of the Dark Gods, and none had ever managed to marshal such a determined campaign of retribution.

The arrival of the Stormcasts marked the beginning of the Realmgate Wars, in which Sigmar's servants sought to control the Realmgates and re-establish alliances with former members of the Pantheon of Order. At first the Slaves to Darkness suffered greatly under this assault. Confronted by enemies who had the crucial advantage of surprise and could match them blow for blow, entire tribes were wiped out in quick succession. Yet cruelty is tenacious. Gradually, the Slaves to Darkness took the measure of their foes. Soon the followers of the Dark Gods won as many battles as they lost, casting their celestial adversaries back to Azyr and earning reward on top of reward from their patron deities.

Archaon led many battles against the Stormcasts, for he rejoiced at the chance to best Sigmar's chosen. In so doing his plan to assault Azyr was put into motion. It was the Everchosen's intent to harness the power of the godbeasts, employing their strength to smash through the gates of the heavens. In this, he was thwarted; the World Titan Behemat was slain by the Stormcasts beneath Ghyran's Great Green Torc, while in the Lands of the Chained Sun, Ignax the Solar Drake – though at first bound to the Everchosen – was released from servitude through a mighty spellbreaker rune wrought into her hide by Fyreslayers of the Austarg lodge. More frustratingly

still, the arcways leading to Ghyran, Aqshy and Ghur were disrupted at the climax of the Realmgate Wars, removing the most efficient means of transporting Archaon's armies to these lands. As free cities of Order began to rise, Archaon sought new methods of conquest. In the meantime, the Everchosen commanded his armies to bring death to the enemies of the gods – not that the glory-hungry champions of Chaos required much encouraging.

VENGEANCE OF THE DEAD

Just as hope had begun to return to the Mortal Realms, Nagash's machinations saw it shattered. Having long since recovered from defeat at the Everchosen's hand, and enraged by the theft of souls he believed rightfully his by his fellow gods, the Great Necromancer set in motion a grand ritual that would transform every realm into an empire of the dead.

Across the realms, the seers and warleaders of the dark tribes were wracked by deathly visions and omens. The mightiest of these was Marakarr Blood-Sky, a Darkoath Warqueen who assembled a colossal multitude of tribes under her banner to march on Nagashizzar and thwart Nagash's plot. Yet even she was unable to stop the ritual in time; only the machinations of the Great Horned Rat prevented the God of the Dead achieving his goal, and even then the result was devastating.

The resulting storm of Shyishan magic that rippled across the realms saw thousands of Nighthaunt spirits rise from their graves, forming great ghostly armies that served as Nagash's vanguard of terror. It also heralded the dawning of the Arcanum Optimar, a time of great magical flux where lingering, predatory manifestations of magic could be summoned to devastate a wizard's enemies – though not necessarily be controlled afterwards.

As the Soul Wars began, the Slaves to Darkness found themselves beset. In a grim irony their success during the Age of Chaos worked against them – in slaughtering so many, they had provided fertile ground for raising vast quantities of Nighthaunt spirits. Armies of shrieking gheists fell upon many warbands, tearing them apart with ethereal claws. The tribes, however, were no strangers to the otherworldly, and soon strove to annihilate the deathless armies. Marakarr and her host – having taken advantage of the upheaval and confusion caused by the necroquake to fight their way clear of the catacombs they had been trapped in during the march on Nagashizzar – had been hardened by their fighting in Shyish, and launched a dark crusade against the malignant armies. Before long, the Mortal Realms rang to the clash of Chaos and Death.

The Eightpoints were not spared from the arcane phenomena sweeping the realms; broken ruins were infested by unquiet spirits, while the corridors of the Varanspire resounded to mournful wailing from unseen sources. The magical flux unleashed by the necroquake reverberated strongly in these lands; before long, predatory manifestations of magic twisted by the power of Chaos terrorised the land. Around the arcway that led to Shyish, strange lights and fell portents were witnessed in great abundance, as if some monstrous power exerted itself on the other side. No warband who passed through the Endgate to investigate ever returned.

Archaon was enraged that he had not foreseen the disaster, that the steady progress of Nagash's plot had evaded the gaze of even the Eye of Sheerian, the artefact that granted Archaon his great prescience. Equally, the necroquake brought with it a realisation; in focusing so much of his attention on Sigmar, Archaon had become blind to those he had thought long defeated. No longer would that be the case. It was time for the Everchosen and his armies to strike back, and to remind the realms why they feared Chaos.

Archaon passed beyond the sight of even his most trusted servants, despatching bands of Varanguard to enforce his will in his absence. The Everchosen drew his nine Gaunt Summoners to his side, and set the daemon-sorcerers a single task. Before the new war could begin, he had an old ally to seek out…

HOSTS OF DAMNATION

The anarchic nature of Chaos makes it almost impossible to apply consistent logic to its armies. There are, however, some common factors that define these legions. Champions who achieve great glory will attract many warriors to their banner, and in turn can be overthrown by one who has risen higher in the favour of the gods.

Most Slaves to Darkness belong to a Horde, an assemblage of warbands and champions under a single master known as the Godsworn Overlord. The term 'warband' is used with little precision by the followers of Chaos. Most simply, it refers to a group of warriors and their ruling champion. In truth however, there is no one definition; it can describe both a handful of Marauders under their tribal chief, and a hundred or more ironclad killers marching at the side of a mighty Daemon Prince. Similarly, a Horde does not require unthinkable numbers to be considered as such by the dark tribes. A tight-knit force of Chosen or Chaos Knights can just as accurately consider themselves a Horde as thousands upon thousands of howling tribesmen, and few who face them in battle would dispute the claim.

Hordes are akin to cults of personality, their warmongering path directed by the whims of the Godsworn Overlord and their inner circle. How these champions choose to walk the Path to Glory, and the aspect of the Chaos Pantheon – if any – that they swear themselves to will ultimately define the composition and tactics of the warbands under their control. Each Horde can, nevertheless, be defined as one of three separate archetypes based on how their masters seek immortality – the Ravagers, the Cabalists and the Despoilers.

Ravager Hordes are the most numerous, having spread across the realms in their lust for conquest. There is often little subtlety to the tactics or aims of the Ravagers, but this is no impediment, for their skilled warriors rejoice in meeting any challenge with cold steel. Those who fall are soon replaced, for many savage tribes are drawn to the warpath of a Ravager Horde, eager to share in the spoils of their pillaging and victories. More so than any other form of Horde, Ravager armies tend to contain many powerful champions vying for control; often these figures possess a shared background, such as the Graven Fang tribe that is ruled by three sister-Warqueens. It is the tragedy of Chaos, however, that eventually these champions must slay one another to ascend the Path to Glory. Only one can rule, and all who stand in a champion's way must be removed, lest divine favour falls on them instead.

The Cabalists seek power through means other than simple slaughter. Their Hordes are led by covens of sorcerers who have studied the secrets of blood magic, enacting dark rituals through the sacrifice of their servants; many originate from the deathly lands of Shyish, where soul-mages and channellers of the dead have long held prominence. Some tribes serve the Cabalists willingly, considering it an honour to feed the gods' hunger with their souls, while others are little more than slaves forced into submission by a sorcerer's chosen followers – or are even controlled like puppets by the warlock cabals. The dawning of the Arcanum Optimar has seen the number of Cabalist Hordes swell, for the manifestation of predatory spells has been of great interest to many sorcerers, and there are those who seek power by mastering or even absorbing this wild magic.

The rarest Hordes are known as the Despoilers. These are amongst the most dreaded armies of the Slaves to Darkness, for in most cases they are led by Daemon Princes – those few champions who have reached the end of the Path to Glory and achieved the immortality they so crave. These beings have returned to command their former warbands – or assemble new armies of the devoted from across the realms – and seek to spread corruption to every corner of creation. Most Despoiler Hordes will contain but one Prince, for these ascended beings are jealous and egotistical almost to a fault. There are, however, some that are ruled by multiple daemons; these are fraught alliances at best, kept intact only through complex webs of competing rivalries and hellish pacts. Where these ruinous beings walk the land cracks and writhes, thick palls of blackness manifesting as the Realm of Chaos seeps into the bedrock of reality. Despoiler Hordes are often smaller than their Ravager and Cabalist equivalents, for only the mightiest can withstand the presence of a Daemon Prince for long. Alongside them lope all manner of hideous, mutated monsters, drawn to the chaotic aura of a Daemon Prince and invigorated by the dark energies that surround them.

When Archaon or one of his favoured lieutenants takes to the field, the disparate Hordes set aside their differences for a time to come together as a single force of untold devastation known as the Host of the Everchosen. Often they will be joined by one of the dreaded circles of the Varanguard riding in force; in some cases entire armies may consist of the Knights of Ruin, unleashed when an enemy has truly earned the Everchosen's ire.

While most assemblages of Slaves to Darkness feature a multitude of minor warbands, each devoted to a different aspect of Chaos, there are some tribes – or even entire Hordes – that have dedicated themselves to just one Ruinous Power. Known as the Godtouched, these warriors all bear their patron's mark; though they have not yet been chosen in the manner of Bloodbound or Arcanites, they have shown promise enough to at least draw the gaze of their god. The divine power that flows through the Godtouched is a source of jealous awe amongst their fellows, and a reward for the intensity of their single-minded devotion.

LORD INFERNIL'S REAVERS

GODSWORN OVERLORD
Magnos Infernil, Butcher of the Cyclopean Span, atop the fearsome Manticore Dreadrend

CHAMPIONS OF RUIN
Lord Infernil surrounds himself with the most skilled warriors of the Horde, veteran Chosen and Knights of the Hellbound Brotherhood, who know that to follow their Godsworn master is to find the greatest opportunities for glory.

GODSWRATH WARBAND OF LORD DORGOTH MURDERBLADE

Many of Murderblade's warriors worship Chaos in the form of the Ever-Falling Axe, and loathe the rampant hedonists of lord Rapcion's court.

RUINBRINGER WARBAND OF LORD EGRIL THE BUTCHER

A veteran of brutal mounted battles waged amongst the Reaver Wastes of Aridian, Egril's many chariot and outrider warbands are the swift hammer-blow of lord Infernil's armies.

FELLRUIN WARBAND OF KYSO THE RED SEER

Having slain Lord Daemonicus and claimed rulership of his warband, the shaman-chief Kyso now plots to wrest control of the Horde entire from Lord Infernil.

PLEASUREBOUND WARBAND OF LORD RAPCION THE DEVOURER

Having fallen entirely into the worship of excess, Rapcion leads six bands of sensation-seeking Godtouched to gratify their most vile desires.

The Horde of Magnos Infernil was once commanded by the mighty Daemon Prince known as Kravoth the Black, the scourge of Lethradel. When Kravoth ascended to fight in the Great Game of the gods, Infernil took control of his armies through strength of arms and cunningly wrought pacts with fellow champions. Now he maintains an iron grip on his Ravagers through a mixture of fear, dark charisma and consistent success in battle, leading them ever-onwards in search of fresh conquest and glory.

Like most Hordes, the warriors and tribes that make up Infernil's Reavers are loosely assembled into warbands based on their cultural background and murderous talents. Infernil's personal enforcers are his Champions of Ruin. These are the warriors closest to the Godsworn Overlord, and it is often from their ranks that a new leader will rise. Godswrath Warbands are the heart of many Hordes, scores of devoted warriors massing around a Warshrine to their patron Power, while Ruinbringer warbands are gatherings of mounted warriors that revel in the hunt and the killing charge. The Godtouched, such as Rapcion's Pleasurebound, are devoted entirely to doing their patron god's will and typically follow a Horde only so long as it suits their immediate aims.

ANNALS OF RUIN

To chronicle even a fraction of the battles fought by the Slaves to Darkness would fill the largest libraries of Azyrheim many times over. Numberless champions have risen and fallen along the Path to Glory demanded by the Dark Gods, and when their armies gather in force the resultant wars scar the very fabric of the Mortal Realms.

● AGE OF MYTH ●

BOUNTY OF THE HEAVENS

Sigmar begins to bring the gifts of civilisation to the tribes of humanity. Gradually, cities are founded across the Mortal Realms, and the Pantheon of Order rules as divine protectors. It is a time of plenty – yet not all of the old ways are forgotten.

WHISPERS FROM BEYOND

As cracks begin to appear in the Pantheon of Order over the course of centuries, growing mortal weakness germinates a seed of darkness that the Gods of Chaos eagerly exploit. In the guise of ancient tribal deities they fuel these negative emotions, drawing many cultures into their worship in return for promises of power. Evil rites are performed in the worship of deities whose names have not been uttered for millennia. The walls of reality grow thinner as the power of Chaos waxes.

REALITY BURSTS

Through their devotion, the faithful of the Dark Gods weaken the barrier between the Mortal Realms and the Realm of Chaos enough for the daemonic legions to burst through. The Pantheon of Order is sent reeling as reality is besieged by the armies of the Ruinous Powers. Millions of mortals pledge themselves to Chaos to avoid being slain by the daemonic hosts, throwing off the shackles of civilisation and becoming the first Slaves to Darkness.

● AGE OF CHAOS ●

THE PATH TO RUIN

The Slaves to Darkness spread across the Mortal Realms as the Age of Chaos rages, slaughtering every civilisation that stands in their way. The first champions step onto the Path to Glory, earning divine rewards for each horrific deed they perform. To mastermind their conquest of reality, the Dark Gods

call upon the Everchosen, promising him dominion over every land ground beneath his heel. Kingdom after kingdom is soon conquered by the Exalted Grand Marshal and his legions.

BURNING SKIES

Upon the Fireplains of Aqshy, the armies of Order, Death and Destruction meet Archaon's hordes in apocalyptic battle. Seven times does Sigmar's charge threaten to win the day, yet the Everchosen has planned for such an eventuality. Upon the eighth assault an illusion conjured by Archaon baits Sigmar into hurling his blessed hammer, Ghal Maraz; it is soon sucked into a wound in reality, hurtling across the cosmos before landing in Chamon. Shorn of his mightiest weapon, Sigmar is forced to retreat, Archaon's laughter ringing in his ears.

ARCHAON TRIUMPHANT

In the wake of the Battle of Burning Skies, the Pantheon of Order is driven into hiding. Sigmar is forced to seal the Gates of Azyr, consigning millions of mortals to death or forcing them to sell their souls to survive. Over the course of the Nexus Wars, Archaon conquers the Allpoints and raises the tower of the Varanspire. Many fallen cultures begin embarking on dark pilgrimages to these cursed lands,

battling for the right to join the Everchosen's conquering armies.

THE ABANDONED

Realising that there can be no victory against the massed hordes of Chaos, King Khalid Kol-Mehn of the Kingdom of Sol leads his people in a desperate flight across Aqshy. They seek one of the fabled Gates of Azyr, behind which the God-King has promised sanctuary from the daemonic onslaught. Pursued and savaged constantly by brazen-hoofed daemons, only a few thousand survivors manage to reach the glittering Realmgate, with baying foes closing in on all sides. Yet just as King Kol-Mehn reaches out for the swirling portal, its light fades and its aura of ancient magic sputters to nothing. Sigmar has closed the Gates of Azyr, and the last sons and daughters of Sol are doomed.

King Kol-Mehn falls to his knees, cursing the God-King's name and offering his soul and those of his people in exchange for a chance at vengeance against the betrayers in Azyr. The Dark Gods hear this plea, and in their capriciousness they decide to answer. Suddenly swollen with unnatural strength, their flesh rippling with profane blessings, Kol-Mehn and his followers turn and slaughter their daemonic pursuers. From that day on the survivors of Sol name themselves the Abandoned, and become amongst the most savage and merciless persecutors of the God-King's faithful.

SMOKE AND BLADES

The Cabalist coven of Malcedex Vos joins the hosts of the Hedonite lord Kalian the Insatiable. Invited into the Slaaneshi champion's mirrorsteel palace, Malcedex's smoke-shrouded illusions dazzle the pleasure-seekers of Kalian's court. Delight turns to horror, however, as the smoky shapes take on physical form; what appeared to be mere illusions are in fact Chaos Knights of the Black Star warband delivered into the palace's heart by Vos's magic. The slaughter that follows is one-sided. By its end Kalian has been torn asunder by Malcedex's followers, while his supplicant tribes are reduced to fodder to fuel the Cabalists' fell rituals.

TAINTED WATERS

The river tribes of northern Invidia successfully drive back a host of Nurgle daemons from their lands, slaying hundreds in a great battle at the Fork of the Minuet. Yet so much Plaguebearer blood is spilled into the life-giving waters of these once pristine waterways that they become clogged and putrescent. Unable to drink the tainted liquid or feed upon the rotting, bloated fish within, the Invidian tribes are stricken by terrible thirst and hunger.

In desperation, they pray to any gods or higher powers that might listen for rainfall, and for sorely needed food. Rotigus the Generous hears their call. The Great Unclean One summons a pestilential downpour of ooze that overflows the banks of the Minuet Rivers and swamps the tribespeople's lands. It brings with it bountiful diseases, mutations and other grotesque blessings. Choosing damnation over obliteration, the survivors of the river tribes finally accept these gifts. Thereafter, they refer to themselves as the Grey Deluge. This pious Ravager Horde travels far and wide, extolling the virtues of its saviour – and slaughtering any who shun the Rainfather's magnanimous offerings.

THE LORD OF PISTONS

Skar'torath, the Monarch of Screams, is banished in Chamon by the armies of Prosperia. Infuriated, the Daemon Prince speaks the Oath of the Iron Pact and is transmuted into a Soul Grinder. Upon re-entering the Golden Realm, Skar'torath finds himself in Chamon's outerlands. The Soul Grinder soon discovers tribes who have gravitated towards the mercurial wastes. Many are slain as Skar'torath seeks to repay the soul-debt owed for his transformation, but he spares those who worship him as an ironclad demigod. Soon the Soul Grinder is on the

warpath back towards the kingdom that defied him, accompanied by hordes of barbarians bearing all manner of mechanical grafts and implantations.

THE BLACK FEAST OF DROM

The duardin kingdom of Drom, nestled amidst the Smoulderpeak mountains of Aqshy, is one of the few civilisations to still stand after centuries of Chaos assaults. Displeased by the resistance of the defenders, Archaon unleashes the Seventh Circle of the Varanguard – the Bane Sons. Riding at the head of a vast mounted host, the Bane Sons trample the gromril-clad throngs sent to stop them. They spare only the Runelords, instead devouring them in a gory feast. Through this cannibalistic rite the Bane Sons gain insight into the runic locks carved upon Drom's Iron Gate. Armed with such knowledge the Varanguard cast down the defences with ease, slaughtering the duardin of Drom and hanging their severed heads upon the shattered Gate.

WHISPERS IN DARKNESS

The seven Shadow Cities of the Simrulas Coast prove stern foes for the armies of the Everchosen. Masters of illusion and subterfuge, the Umbral Lords of those darkling strongholds lure the attacking Ravager Hordes into a series of terrible slaughters. It is only through the machinations of Be'lakor the First Prince that the Shadow Cities at last succumb. Whispering promises of salvation to each lord should they turn upon their fellows, Be'lakor weaves a complex web of intrigue,

murder and torment that brings his enemies to their knees. Paranoid and fearful of their kin as much as the invading hosts massing upon their borders, the Umbral Lords prove easy prey when Be'lakor finally sends forth his daemonic legions. They tear each Shadow City apart in turn, gleefully devouring the souls of the occupants and raising statues woven from shadow in honour of their Dark Master.

WAR OF THE THIGHBONE

The Ravager Horde of Gnarl Shatterskull becomes embroiled in a brutal war with Bonesplitter orruks of the Bonegrinz Warclan when he steals the sacred relic they call Grummok's Leg – the thighbone of a gargantuan Magma Dragon slain by a hero of the orruks in ages past that grants ferocious bestial strength to all who lay their hands upon it. Slaughtering each other with abandon across the peaks of the Hungry Mountain in Ghur, the two foes stain the snowy heights crimson with gore. In the following centuries, Grummok's Leg changes hands a hundred times, and the bloodshed shows no sign of abating.

GIFT OF MUTATION

Upon the remote island of Din in Chamon, warlike tribes worship an immense Mutalith Vortex Beast that dwells within a cavern filled with streams of molten silver and geysers of bubbling flesh. Rival tribesmen and other prisoners captured by the Dinese are given to the creature as sacrifices. Most are devoured or transmuted into pillars of screaming crystal or other hideous forms. A rare few are granted the great honour of being transformed into mewling, tentacled and half-metallic Chaos Spawn. The Dinese call these fortunates the Silver-Blessed, and follow them into battle reverently.

THE FURYSWARM

Thousands of Chaos Furies gather together in an immense flock, sweeping across the plains of Aqshy like a plague of cruel locusts and slaughtering all in their path. Many tribes and kingdoms fall before the swarm of lesser daemons disperses as suddenly and mysteriously as it formed.

HARADH'S REBELLION

With Archaon once again absent from the Eightpoints, the immense Chaos Gargant known as Haradh the Breaker dares to rise against the Varanspire, claiming that he alone is worthy of usurping the Everchosen's crown. Haradh gathers great numbers of Fomoroid Crushers to his side, promising them freedom if they helped bring down the Dreadholds which they once slaved away to build. Haradh's host makes it as far as the gates of the Citadel of Ruin itself before the Three-Eyed King and the Varanguard of his Third Circle descend upon them – a distant ruler he may be, but no hint of rebellion within his domain escapes the Exalted Grand Marshal's notice. Haradh's army is slaughtered, and the gargant flees to his mountaintop fortress. Archaon pursues him, and in a swift yet brutal battle, carves open Haradh the Breaker's belly with the Slayer of Kings, and stakes him out to die a slow and agonising death beneath the pitiless skies of the Eightpoints. Thereafter, the mountaintop site of the traitor's painful demise is known as Haradh's Torment.

THE GLORY OF NOCHSEED

Even as many of its Hyshian neighbours are consumed by infernal flames, the gleaming ziggurat-city of Nochseed still stands proud and unblemished. Its masked rulers put themselves forth as beings of culture and honour holding out against the darkness, but rumours persist that they practise vile rituals within the depths of their temples, and that it was in fact their spies that arranged the downfall of their closest rivals by making pacts with mysterious, daemonic patrons.

⚫ AGE OF SIGMAR ⚫

THE GOD-KING RETURNS

The Age of Sigmar begins in a flash of lightning. From the heavens, the Stormcast Eternals return to the Mortal Realms to unleash Sigmar's vengeance. Hundreds of Slaves to Darkness tribes are slaughtered in the initial onslaught, though the servants of Chaos soon begin to take the measure of their celestial foes.

A GRISLY GAMBIT

Deep within the jungles of Invidia, the ogor warglutt known as the Craw threatens the rituals of the sorcerer Garathrax. Knowing of the Craw's terrifying reputation, the fatesworn Cabalist negotiates a deal with the Splintered Fang tribe, promising prime alchemical ingredients torn from ogor flesh in return for their aid. When the Craw arrive, they rip through the sorcerer's hosts, though many fall to the spells of Garathrax and his minions. As the cabal flees at battle's end, the ogors feast on the fallen Chaos worshippers. They soon realise their mistake as the slow-acting poison brewed by the Splintered Fang – and that Garathrax has infected his own warriors with – wracks their innards. Even the fearsome constitution of the Craw cannot resist the insidious toxins. As the last ogor chokes on their own bile, Garathrax's callous deception – the latest in a line spanning decades – sees him rise to daemonhood by the will of Tzeentch.

TO TAME A GODBEAST

Throughout the Realmgate Wars – in which the Stormcast Eternals seek to gain control of the Realmgate network – Archaon leads many battles against Sigmar's chosen. At Mount Kronus he slaughters the Hammerhands to a man, yet Archaon has grander plans in mind; freeing the daemon-oracle Kiathanus from its prison, the Everchosen gains knowledge of how to bind the zodiacal godbeasts to his cause. Archaon despatches his minions to claim Ignax the Solar Drake and Behemat the World Titan, seeking their power to breach Azyr. Ultimately, the Everchosen is thwarted by the Stormcasts, though they are forced to unleash the power of the legendary Great Bolts to slay Behemat. Frustrated in his ambitions and incensed by the subsequent loss of several Allgates, Archaon begins to seek new means of conquest.

MASTER OF THE PITS

Archaon grants the Ogroid Myrmidon Skaraggos Split-Eye the title of Grand Pitmaster, after witnessing the creature single-handedly slay a Skitterstrand Arachnarok in the arena. This lofty title grants Skaraggos power over every blood-pit and arena of slaughter in the Eightpoints.

CIVILISATION UNDER SIEGE

The Season of War begins as the forces of Order attempt to consolidate the gains made during the Realmgate Wars. Cities are founded across the innerlands of many realms, particularly Ghyran, where the trio of settlements known as the Seeds of Hope are established in the Everspring Swathe. Many Slaves to Darkness, especially the far-ranging Ravagers, take umbrage with this resurgence of Order and descend upon these nascent cities to cast them down in the name of the Ruinous Powers. Ultimately they fail to overthrow the Seeds of Hope, though the Ironsoul Horde successfully annihilates the burgeoning Ghurish city of Matarka, salting the earth with the spilt blood of the defenders.

FURY OF THE DEAD

Nagash's darkling scheme to engulf every realm in the power of Shyish nears fruition. Many champions receive god-given visions driving them to Shyish; greatest of these is the Darkoath Warqueen Marakarr Blood-Sky. She swiftly assembles a vast horde around the battle-hardened core of her own tribe, absorbing many other warbands by slaughtering their leaders. Blood-Sky nearly succeeds in reaching Nagashizzar and halting Nagash's ambitions, but is waylaid at the last minute by a force of puritanical Stormcast Eternals. Nagash's necroquake ripples across reality as his grand ritual reaches its climax, summoning the spirits of the dead back to the Mortal Realms – though Marakarr survives, and swears to one day shatter Nagashizzar stone by stone.

A LINGERING PUNISHMENT
Across the realms, Nighthaunt spirits rise to assail the living. The Slaves to Darkness eagerly meet the gheists in battle, for even such stark reminders of mortality struggle to unsettle those who dwell in the nightmarish dominion of Chaos. The Despoiler horde of Lavarious the Adulated takes particular glee in the return of these lost souls. His monstrous horde seeks out past battlefields where those who would not bow before them were slaughtered, the Daemon Prince revelling in the opportunity to best his enemies a second time as they rise to take their revenge.

TREASURES UNEARTHED
In the aftermath of the necroquake, a bow wave of raw magic gushes across the realms. In its wake, many ancient secrets are revealed, the illusions and enchantments that protected them for centuries unmade in an instant. Foremost amongst these newly unveiled mysteries are the Stormvaults – arcane repositories constructed by the God-King, and filled with all manner of forbidden secrets. Eager to claim these Stormvaults as their own, the Dark Gods grant many of their most powerful worshippers visions of the plunder and glory that awaits within. Ravager Hordes, Cabalists and Daemon Princes of the Despoilers alike descend upon the Stormvaults, but they soon discover that they are not the only ones to seek out the God-King's treasure chambers.

THE BLACK TOURNEY
Seeking the fiercest killers in the realms, Archaon decrees that a great contest of blood shall take place before the walls of the Varanspire. The Black Tourney matches the greatest Chaos Knights and beast-riding lords against one another in duels to the death, with the prize being a place within the vaunted ranks of the Everchosen's

Varanguard. Thousands of warriors from across the realms travel to the Eightpoints to test their lances against one another; they include rotting chevaliers from the Order of the Fly, black-plated Skullriders from the steppes of Penultima, glittering Knights of the Crack'd Mirror and countless others besides.

Across the sulphurous plains of the Eightpoints, these riders clash in increasingly brutal and bloody battles before a watching audience of Daemon Princes and Chaos Lords – the Three-Eyed King himself is not present, but none doubt that he is aware of each gory death and each act of vicious brutality perpetrated by the contestants. Soon the ground is littered with ripped and torn corpses, and stained dark red with spilled blood. After many days of carnage Desrachus of the Pale Heart triumphs, thrusting the splintered haft of his glaive through the eye of Krasmus Throatcutter. He is granted the honour of joining the Fourth Circle of the Varanguard, the dreaded Reavers of Chaos, and a glorious saga of slaughter and ruin commences.

A FEAST OF SECRETS
The Platinum Spire in Chamon is a particularly large and heavily contested Stormvault, where acid-etched metal tomes filled with studies on dark magic, necromancy and daemon binding are kept in teetering slab-stacks as tall as ironoak trees. A trio of Mindstealer Sphiranxes seeks out this bounty of illicit knowledge, but soon find themselves assailed by warriors of

the Secretkeepers – a Sacrosanct Chamber of the Hallowed Knights. The Stormcast Eternals have come to safeguard the God-King's hidden repository, but the Sphiranxes have no intention of relinquishing their prize. Drawing many Chaos tribes and Tzaangor Shamans to their side via threats, psychic domination and promises of power, they transform the Platinum Spire into a killing ground of illusions, mind-sapping glyphs and sorcerous deathtraps that, try as they might, the Secretkeepers cannot penetrate.

THE STOLEN SKULLS
The Ravagers known as the Blood Revenants make a pilgrimage across the Great Parch of Aqshy each season to pray and offer sacrifice before immense skull-ziggurats. Korghos Khul himself – master of the Goretide and favoured champion of Khorne – raised these towering piles. To the Slaves to Darkness, such sites are sacred places, and thus they are outraged beyond reason when they discover that lumbering Gothizzar Harvesters of the Crematorians have begun to haul away great loads of the bleached skulls for their own macabre ends. The Blood Revenants launch an all-out assault upon the Ossiarch Bonereapers, who respond by sending forth vast hosts of their own volatile, flaming Mortek Guard. With axe and blade the Crematorians are finally driven off, but not before they have claimed a fitting tithe of bones – including many freshly slain Blood Revenants.

THE HAUNTED VARANSPIRE
The shock wave of the necroquake reaches even the Eightpoints, the morbid energy of Shyish clashing with the raw power of Chaos. From eerie phantasmal mists emerge the vengeful spirits of those slain in centuries past by the Slaves to Darkness, presenting the battling warbands of the Eightpoints with a new and deadly challenge. Strange lights and deathly phenomena are observed with increasing regularity around the arcway that leads to Shyish. With their master absent, Archaon's garrison-lords begin to prepare their defences against whatever threat is coming…

ARCHAON THE EVERCHOSEN

Amongst the Champions of Chaos, Archaon stands alone. He is the Exalted Grand Marshal of the Apocalypse, the favoured of the pantheon, and by his command are the Mortal Realms remade in the image of Chaos. Behind him the armies of the Ruinous Powers march as one, forged into a single terrifying force by the will of the Everchosen.

Every worshipper or beast of Chaos that walks, slithers or lopes owes obeisance to Archaon. He is less a man than he is a demigod of the Dark Powers, the chosen commander of their infernal hosts. Yet the Everchosen is no mere puppet. He has earned his position through might, cunning and a sheer determination that has seen the doom of entire worlds. Should the Chaos Gods ever achieve their conquest of the Mortal Realms, it will almost certainly be in large part due to Archaon.

Archaon's origins are shrouded in mystery. Few are the souls who know the truth of his past. In the time of the world-that-was, Archaon bore a different name, and fought as a devout templar of Sigmar. Upon reading the apocalyptic writings of the prophet Necrodomo, he learned a terrible truth concerning the divinity of the Heldenhammer that shattered his every certainty. Taking the name Archaon, he swore to attain the mantle of Everchosen and take his vengeance upon his former lord. Across the realms, however, other tales have spread concerning Archaon. Some believe that he was a great Azyrite emperor who ruled before the coming of Sigmar, and who swore himself to Chaos

to match the power of the upstart God-King. Many tribes believe that Archaon is simply a manifestation of the Dark Powers – that when Chaos came into being, so did their greatest champion. The tribes of the Untamed Beasts honour him as the Eater of Worlds, while the shadowy Corvus Cabal see him as an avatar of their avaricious daemon-god, the Great Gatherer.

Archaon's almighty status is demonstrated through his bearing of the legendary artefacts known as the Six Treasures of Chaos. These are no mere trinkets; each is an ancient item steeped in terrible power, and that marks his status as Everchosen. Upon Archaon's brow burns the Mark of Chaos Ascendant, that rarest of sigils denoting the favour of all the gods. Within a groove upon the Crown of Domination sits the Eye of Sheerian, ripped from the belly of the Chaos Dragon known as Flamefang and which grants the Everchosen a degree of foresight – a fact that, combined with Archaon's tactical brilliance, makes him nearly impossible to outmanoeuvre in battle. The Armour of Morkar is almost impervious to blows, and was once worn by the first to bear the mantle of Everchosen in the depths of pre-history. Perhaps

most infamous of these artefacts is the Slayer of Kings. Within this legendary blade is the essence of the daemon U'zhul, who delights – and excels – in devouring the souls of monarchs and champions.

Though he fights their wars and leads their armies, the Gods of Chaos regard Archaon with a measure of unease – perhaps even fear. They are right to do so. Each of the Brothers in Darkness has attempted to sway the Everchosen to their exclusive service, and each has failed, the most powerful of their servants slain by Archaon or ripped apart by his monstrous mount, Dorghar. Within the abyssal reaches of his soul, there is a part of Archaon – or perhaps the man he once may have been – that looks upon the machinations of all deities, whether they are one of Sigmar's failed pantheon or his own supposed masters, with contempt. Many of those sworn to Chaos bear the Everchosen's brand above any of the dark pantheon. There are those who whisper that should Archaon ever achieve his ultimate aim of grinding the Mortal Realms beneath his heel, there will be no gods to play games with the lives of mortals – nothing, save the black banners of the Everchosen raised across the length and breadth of every realm.

DORGHAR, STEED OF THE APOCALYPSE

The fourth treasure claimed by the Everchosen was the daemonic steed known as Dorghar. The quest for this beast took Archaon into the Realm of Chaos itself, for Dorghar was once the most prized specimen in the menagerie of the daemon lord Agrammon. Infiltrating Agrammon's palace through cunning and guile, Archaon used the Eye of Sheerian to locate Dorghar's cage. Leaping onto the daemon's back, Archaon broke the creature in a titanic contest of wills, binding Dorghar through sheer force of personality – and by offering his new steed the chance to take bloody revenge on his gaolers.

When the Gods of Chaos – save absent Slaanesh – sent some of the mightiest of their greater daemons to test the Everchosen's prowess, Archaon and his mount soon shattered the challengers. Upon drinking the essence from their carcasses Dorghar gained his three heads, each bearing the powers of one of the gods. The fell sorcery that runs through Dorghar's veins also ensures that those he consumes never truly die, meaning that the Steed of the Apocalypse is particularly dreaded by the Stormcast Eternals. Those of their number devoured in battle by Dorghar – such as Thostos Bladestorm, Lord-Celestant of the Celestial Vindicators and hero of the Realmgate Wars – cannot return to Azyr to be reforged, but are instead subjected to an eternity of torment in the creature's stomach.

THE VARANGUARD

Perhaps one in a thousand champions will possess sufficient strength to undertake the trials of the Varanguard. Of these, one in ten thousand may prove themselves worthy to join Archaon's elite. Known as the Knights of Ruin, they are amongst the most feared warriors of Chaos. When they ride in force, even the gods take notice.

To look upon the Varanguard is to witness the Everchosen's wrath made manifest. Each is a mighty champion and conquering warlord in their own right, though they have set aside their dark empires and former lives to ascend to glory at the side of the Everchosen. For Archaon to unleash even a fraction of his Varanguard in their terrible splendour is to sign the death warrant of any who oppose them, for the Knights of Ruin are pitiless in ensuring the Everchosen's commands are carried out.

On occasion, a Champion of Chaos will witness a strange omen as they walk the Path to Glory. Its exact form may vary; the champion may behold the Everchosen's mark amidst a raging inferno, or the spray of blood from a foe's slit artery may form a silhouette of Archaon. From that moment the champion has been singled out by the Three-Eyed King. Some attempt to deny the calling, but few can resist for long. Their dreams are filled with visions nightmarish enough to shake even the most brutal killer, while their bodies are afflicted with wounds that bleed black, oily smoke and which never heal until the chosen accepts their destiny. The Walk of Blades, the Dark Choosing, the Black Labours – these are just some of the titles given to the tests each aspirant must face. There is no telling what these trials will constitute; all that is certain is that a champion must triumph in eight such endeavours, and each will be specially suited to they who undertake it. Most fall during their first trial, for Archaon has no use for any but the strongest. The few who succeed find themselves raised to glory as one of the Varanguard.

Upon completing their trials, a Varanguard is placed into one of the Eight Circles in accordance with their strengths and demeanour. Every Circle is different, invested with their own talents and rituals in much the same manner as a mortal knightly order. Most feared are the Swords of Chaos, those black-armoured lords of the First Circle who have ridden at Archaon's side since time immemorial. From great rents torn in the skies they ride upon a carpet of raw Chaos, crashing into the foe alongside their master with terminal force. As the centuries have passed, however, other Circles have attained their own infamy. The Third Circle, known as the Scions of Darkness, dwell within the most gloom-shrouded chambers of the Varanspire and ride out from palls of unearthly shadow. The Scourges of Fate, the feared headhunters of the Fifth Circle, hang the severed skulls of their prey from the armour of their mutated steeds. Strangest of all

are the Eighth Circle, for even other Varanguard know almost nothing of these nameless warriors – only that none can hope to escape their wrath.

The Varanguard have been instrumental in many of Archaon's greatest campaigns. They were the first to set foot in the Allpoints at the commencement of the Nexus Wars. At Mount Kronus, the Swords of Chaos crushed the Hammerhands Warrior Chamber in its entirety. Should Archaon succeed in smashing down the gates of Azyr, it will be the Varanguard that lead the war to burn Sigmar's realm to cinders. Yet not every battle fought by these knights is a realm-shaking conflict. Archaon despatches bands of Varanguard to carry his will to many different armies of Chaos, and on rare occasions will command a dozen or so to undertake a particularly vital quest. Many Varanguard will have sworn their souls to one of the dark pantheon before receiving the Everchosen's summons, and still possess the blessings of their god. This is not to say that their fellow devoted can manipulate the Varanguard; their loyalty is to Archaon above all, and any believed to stand between the Everchosen and his goals will be annihilated without hesitation.

Since the eruption of the necroquake, the Varanguard have been seen riding across the Mortal Realms with greater regularity – for though the Everchosen is engaged on his own mysterious mission, his command over the armies of Chaos remains absolute. Some Varanguard fight with, or even command, forces such as Bloodbound Warhordes or Arcanite cults, much to the consternation of the lords who formerly held dominance – those who were not simply slain for questioning the will of the Everchosen, that is. The greatest proportion of Varanguard, however, still wage war alongside the Slaves to Darkness. At their command the Hordes assail the boundaries of civilisation with relentless fervour, and on those occasions when Archaon is sighted across the realms, the armies that fight at his beck and call are inevitably spearheaded by a ruinous host of Varanguard from one of the Eight Circles.

MARK OF THE EVERCHOSEN

Should one of the Slaves to Darkness exhibit sufficient brutality and cunning before Archaon or one of his Varanguard, they may be granted the right to bear the icon of the Everchosen himself. This symbol is recognised across the realms as a portent of doom, and is branded onto the favoured warrior by the burning blade of the Slayer of Kings. Many Varanguard bear this mark somewhere on their armour as a mark of prowess, as well as to prove to those who would seek to twist their loyalty that their souls are sworn as much to the Everchosen as to any of the Dark Gods.

KNIGHT OF THE FIFTH CIRCLE

The Varanguard are figures of dreaded legend in the annals of the Mortal Realms. Each is a lord amongst the damned, empowered by the gods and sworn to the service of the Everchosen. Their road to glory is inevitably long and blood-soaked, and where they ride, no foe can stand before them.

He is a child, too young to wage war but old enough to learn the ways of the hunt.

His first kill is with a sling, bringing down a speckled gryphak on the wing. His father shows him how to preserve the bird's flesh in salted strips for the next long journey across the plains, and his shaman teaches him how to crush the bones into powder, to breathe in and induce intoxicating dreams. The beast's feathers, dappled blue and gold, he gives to his mother for her headdress. The creature's inedible claws are woven into his first deed-necklace.

His proudest moment comes with the following dawn, as he recovers from the twitching dreams of the reagent-infused bone powder. His sister, her skin scaled in the warpaint of the tribe's spear-dancers, paints his face with a hunter's woad, marking him as a provider for the kin-clan.

The years pass. He is a young hunter at the precipice of manhood.

His face reflects this, painted with the markings of a killer of beasts, not a slayer of men. There is honour in this. Great honour. But no glory.

And like so many youths of his tribe, he needs one and craves the other. Honour is a necessity, something he desires. But glory? Glory is a thing to thirst for. To kill for. To die for.

He moves through the bracken forest, his footfalls scarcely disturbing the ashy soil, his bare shoulders never brushing the dry and leafless branches. He imagines himself wraith-silent; not like the tormented spectres of the unsleeping dead, but true-silent, making no more sound than a shadow.

In one hand he holds a javelin tipped with red bronze; in the other, a sheath of mottled javik-leather, tied tight and wrapped around two spares.

Three casts. If he can't bring down his prey in three casts, he will have nothing left but a knife of beaten bronze and, may the Vulture God help him, his wits.

Disaster has descended upon his kin-band, and it has fallen to him to break the curse. An oath was sworn, made with blood and spit and fire, that he wouldn't return without seeing it done. Already he regrets leaving his horse behind, but his steed is in heat, making her fractious and unquiet. He needs to hunt in silence tonight, and so he moves on foot, alone in the dead forest.

He sees his prey before it sees him. The figure hunches in a feral squat, eating raw flesh from the throat of an ulayak greatstag. The stag's knuckly antlers shiver with the motions of its defiled corpse, their ivory tips gouging the worthless earth. No steam rises from its open wounds, even on a night this cold. It has been dead for some time, and the creature feasting on its flesh cares nothing for the fact it dines on spoiling meat.

The hunter moves closer, feeling a chill on his skin that has nothing to do with the night air. Sweat makes jewels on his brow, each droplet a diamond threatening to reflect the moonlight. The prey, however, has its back to him. The hunter was careful to ghost around to the rear.

He makes ready now, notching his javelin into an atlatl cane to hurl the dart with far greater strength and speed. With a spear, he can spike a horse on the run, lancing its flank. With an atlatl to add vigour to the cast, he can bring down a stallion with a single heart-strike.

The hunter makes his throw. The moment it flies from his hand, he knows the cast is perfect. He barely even sees it in flight – one moment the dart is launched, the next it's spiked through, jutting from the back of the prey's neck and lanced through the throat.

A perfect throw. A killing cast. A warrior struck by such a hurl wouldn't even have time to gargle any last words; they'd be dead before they had the chance, bereft of vocal cords, breath, and blood to the brain.

Now the prey lies dead, neck-snapped and impaled atop its cold meal. The hunter's fear gives way to pride. That was surely the cast of his young life.

He's murmuring his thanks to the Vulture God when the prey gets to its feet. The prayer fades first to a whisper, and then to nothing. Bloodless sinews creak as the prey turns its head on a broken neck.

Shock steals the hunter's grace. He goes for his spares, drawing the second dart with more panic than haste. The prey comes for him, shambling, stumbling over the uneven earth, and in that moment it ceases being it and becomes her. Even worse, it ceases being prey and becomes someone he knew. Someone he knows.

He says his mother's name. If the dead thing remembers her name, she shows no sign. Her rotting senses track him unerringly. Sightless eyes see exactly where he stands. The God of the Dead blesses those he brings back; this is a lesson the hunter has been told many times around the tribal fires, and now he finally learns the truth of it.

His second cast flies almost as true as the first. It takes her in the heart, breaking her ribs with a dry-branch snap, but the wound is meaningless to the figure of cold bone and cursed meat.

He makes his third cast as she's reaching for him, and Fate – or Fate's misbegotten child, Luck – is on his side at last. The dart drives through the gravewalker's eye with enough force to stagger her, and the hunter bears her stumbling form to the ground.

Hands that have been dead for days claw bluntly at his face. He closes his eyes so she can't gouge them out and he does what he came to do, avenging the hex placed upon his family by sawing through the dead woman's neck with his flensing knife.

Three days later the hunter rejoins his tribe. He casts the ghoulish trophy before his warchief as the spear-dancers gather by the revel fires, and over his mother's severed head he declares himself a breaker of curses, a blooded warrior, a child no more.

The years unspool, and he is as much a myth as a man.

Glory has brought him this far, and glory drives him still. He is a blood-shedder, a life-reaver, a knight of the True Gods who has carved a legend in the flesh of his foes with the lance in his hand.

He is also scarred, and aching, and saturated with spite accrued over centuries.

The battle rages around him, drenching him in the din of metal on metal, men and women screaming to maintain their exhausted rage. The air stinks of blood and scorched iron and the filth that runs from the bodies of the slain. Horns sound

above the ceaseless melee, plaintive and wayward, inspiring men forward or commanding retreats. The sun beats down upon both armies, baking the ironclad warriors and the Ghurish wilderness around them as they crash and clash and sweat and bleed and die.

The knight pays heed to none of this. For years he fought in the press of shield on shield, hacking with blades until they blunted, thrusting with spears until they broke. Those days of fear and fury are long behind him now.

Artauroth rears beneath him, its warped jaws parted in a roar both ursine and canine as it lashes out with nail-shod hooves. The knight feels his companion's war-joy, a physical aura around the roaring creature, but he hauls on the reins, forcing them both clear of the chaos, refusing to be drawn into the battle.

Even after centuries, fighting that temptation is harder, not easier. His tongue tingles with blood-need, his muscles sting with unspent strength – the knight knows his presence in the front lines would break hundreds of foes, but the Three-Eyed King demanded only one thing of him this day. That lone commandment cannot be achieved if the knight loses himself to the narcotic taste of battle-madness.

He spurs clear and rides on. Just as the creature he sits astride is no longer a horse, the knight is no longer just a man. His face is forever hidden behind a brazen helm; his flesh is sealed beneath ancient rune-marked plate. When he rides, his daemonic steed's hooves eat at the earth like acid.

No one has spoken his true name in centuries. In truth, the knight has forgotten it himself. Even his allies greet him by title; dread has instilled a sense of formality within even these barbaric souls, and when they come before him, their tattooed mouths shape the word 'Varanguard'.

There... He sees his prey across the field of battle. There! A crested duardin, armed with axes of silver and armoured in gold; a king of these wretched things, if they can even be said to have kings. The high

sun dagger-flashes off the metal runes hammered into the duardin's skin. The stunted creature's face is red with the effort of crying out for the aid of his ancestors.

In moments like this, the knight becomes the hunter once more, and cruel spurs fang their way into Artauroth's hide. The horse-creature leaps forward at a dead run, the gallop seamlessly becoming a charge. Rider and steed plunge through the battle-dust kicked up by ten thousand feet, reining around the slow infantry when they can, slaughtering their way through where they must.

The duardin king turns. This squat figure of rippling muscle and plaited beard-hair and whirling axes – he turns and sees death riding closer. He raises his blades to the knight.

The knight lowers his lance, aiming the barbed tip at the doomed lord.

The moment of truth, when it comes, lasts for several blade-breaking, blood-gouting minutes. Yet it ends as they all end: with a lance driven through armour and flesh and bone, through a champion's heart.

As dusk falls, the knight rejoins the warhost. He casts the trophy to the tainted earth as the funeral pyres burn, and over the severed head of a duardin warlord, the Knight of the Fifth Circle faces down the warleaders of seven tribes. Their war is won, just as the knight promised. The enemy king is slain, just as the knight vowed.

At dawn the next day, the horde rides the plains, making haste to reach Archaon's side and the great gathering that awaits. But the Varanguard does not lead them. He abandons them, his duty done.

As he rides alone, he touches the talisman at his mailed throat, where a set of timeworn gryphak claws rest against his armour. The gesture is a habit now, a thing of repetition through emotionless compulsion, the way some of the unquiet dead will haunt the places of their murder.

The nameless knight rides west, towards the lands that lie near the realm's edge. Archaon's will demands it, for there he will find other beasts to butcher, other tribes to bind, and other kings to slay.

WARLORDS OF THE DARK TRIBES

The warlords of Chaos are bringers of ruin and devastation, each blessed many times over by the gods and commanding hundreds or even thousands of lesser warriors. For these champions, the ultimate reward is but a few steps away, and they will allow nothing to stop them from attaining the favour of the Dark Gods.

CHAOS LORDS

Chaos Lords are the masters and champions of the Slaves to Darkness Hordes. Their names are whispered in fear amongst the civilised lands, and the carnage they wreak across the realms has shifted the course of history on more than one occasion. To rise to this vaunted rank is to stand only a step away from eternal glory or eternal damnation. Every Chaos Lord knows that the eyes of the gods are upon them, and their determination to prove their might to the dark pantheon makes them terrible foes to face indeed.

There is no single moment that marks the ascension of a champion to a Chaos Lord; rather, they will eventually rise to rulership of their people by virtue of their skill and strength. Some Hordes, particularly those made up of multiple tribes, contain numerous exemplars favoured enough to be considered Chaos Lords. Each will be in constant competition with their rivals, seeking to prove their might and claim the position of Godsworn Overlord – and the divine favour that accompanies it.

In order to maintain their pre-eminent position in the gaze of the gods, Chaos Lords must constantly seek to perform great deeds to prove their might. The dark rewards they have gained over the course of their lives ensures that a Chaos Lord is far stronger and swifter than a normal man, and hard-won experience has honed their skills to a razor edge. There is no challenge a Chaos Lord will shirk from; they will stand in the path of a frenzied troggoth and deal the beast such a blow that it is knocked immediately into unconsciousness, or duel with daemonic champions in return for power or knowledge – putting their very souls on the line in return. A Chaos Lord's weapons are just as dangerous as the warrior who wields them. Many of these cursed blades or wicked flails contain the bound essence of daemons, and while these beings rage at their confinement – and will take any chance to slip free of their bounds – their destructive power means most Chaos Lords are willing to risk their wrath.

Champions who particularly impress the gods may find themselves bequeathed a daemonic mount. These beings can take any shape that pleases them and their master, from iron-scaled serpents to huge flame-snorting destriers. Such strong-willed and vicious beasts pose a constant threat to their master, but this is considered just one more challenge a Chaos Lord must overcome to prove their worth. Still, some Chaos Lords prefer to place their trust in a more natural, though just as deadly, creature known as a Karkadrak. These reptilian brutes were once natives of the Allpoints, though have since spread to every realm save Azyr. Their scales are as hard as rock, their durability often further bolstered by plates of hellforged iron. In turn, armour is little protection against the tearing horn of a Karkadrak. When one of these brutes goes on the rampage, it is almost impossible to stop; only a Lord who can halt the creature's deadly momentum can force the Karkadrak to submit to them.

By far the most ferocious beast ridden to war by the Chaos Lords, however, is the Manticore. These leonine creatures are so thoroughly suffused with the power of Chaos that their only true point of commonality is sheer fury. So primal is the wrath of a Manticore that at least one Greatfray of the Beasts of Chaos worships them as avatars of pure Chaos. Manticores are fiercely territorial, and will attack anything that enters their hunting grounds with unthinking savagery. Most Chaos Lords who attempt to dominate a Manticore are soon shredded for their troubles, but a rare few succeed in battling the creature to a standstill and proving themselves the apex predator. These iron-willed overlords are roundly feared by those under their command, for to defy them is death – either on the end of the Chaos Lord's blade, or more commonly by being torn apart by their Manticore's sharpened claws.

EXALTED HEROES

Exalted Heroes are champions who have begun to attract the notice of the gods but not yet risen to the vaunted rank of Chaos Lord. While their Path to Glory may be just beginning, only a fool would underestimate them. A single Exalted is equal to a score of lesser men, and their determination to gain godly favour sees them take on any challenge without hesitation. More practically, Exalted Heroes tend to possess warbands of followers, who seek to bask in the champion's reflected glory. This makes attracting the service of Exalted Heroes crucial to any Chaos Lord seeking to swell the ranks of their Horde. They often act as enforcers for the Godsworn Overlord, leading their warriors on pillaging raids or using their martial skills to anchor a battleline.

Whether they worship a single aspect of the Ruinous Powers or instead devote themselves to Chaos Undivided, Exalted Heroes are forces to be reckoned with. They believe that only by triumphing over the greatest foes can they achieve the greatest renown. In the Chaos-dominated wilds of the realms, the most common enemies faced by an Exalted Hero are rival champions – duels in which the Exalted can prove their god's supremacy even as they add the defeated champion's warriors to their warband. An Exalted reserves the most loathing, however, for those who seek to oppose the gods. Such foes are hacked down in a whirlwind of blows, their defences no match for the merciless fury of the Exalted. When an enemy commander lies defeated, an Exalted Hero will use a ritual dagger to carve out the enemy's heart, holding the gory trophy aloft and beseeching the Dark Gods to grant them a reward.

DARKOATH WARLEADERS

The Darkoath are an enigma, yet one that has already had a lasting effect on the tribes and cultures of the Slaves to Darkness. Even the most far-sighted sorcerers cannot divine precisely from where they emerged, or which tribe was the first to see these warriors rise to power. All that can be said for certain is that from their earliest appearance, these warriors have been possessed of a relentless focus and a lust for conquest that exceeds that of all but the most strong-willed Chaos Lords. Clad in thick furs and wielding weapons etched with runes of death and bloodshed, the warleaders of the Darkoath command the barbarous tribes with a unity and strength of purpose that makes amongst the most dangerous foes of civilisation.

The Darkoath are named after their practice of swearing great oaths to the Dark Gods, recording these pacts upon graven stone tablets. Though it is not unusual for a champion to offer pledges to their patron, the regularity with which the Darkoath make such vows and fulfil them has become infamous. Though they often receive blessings that amplify their killing potential, the Darkoath do not swear themselves to any one god. This partly explains how they are able to attract so many boons; that any group of warriors could resist dedicating their souls to a single patron for so long infuriates the Brothers in Darkness to no end, and – though they would never admit it – the Chaos Gods desire these strong, unclaimed souls so much so that they will offer the greatest of rewards in an effort to sway the Darkoath.

Tribes with a high proportion of barbarous Marauders are particularly favoured by the Darkoath, and in turn are eager to follow these champions into battle; as such, it is the Hordes of the

Ravagers that include the greatest number of Darkoath. Though they bear a similar philosophy concerning how to attract the favour of the gods, there is little unity amongst the ranks of the Darkoath. As always with the Champions of Chaos, mastery is assured through having the strength to impose one's will. The greatest Darkoath have yoked vast numbers of tribesmen to their cause, whipping them into a frenzy as they drive them into battle. That many will fall is of no concern to the Darkoath. After all, sacrifices must always be made to ensure their oaths to the gods are kept.

Darkoath Chieftains are skilled warriors who rule their supplicant tribes with an iron fist. The Darkoath Warqueens, meanwhile, are the leaders of entire Hordes. The pacts sworn and fulfilled by these supreme fighters have seen

them rewarded with plentiful dark blessings, rendering them stronger and swifter than any normal human. These gifts are alloyed with a natural charisma that allows a Warqueen to unite many tribes into a single unstoppable force when the gods demand it. Perhaps the most dangerous quirk of the Warqueens are the strange visions that afflict them. Ever since the Time of Tribulations, Warqueens have experienced vivid dreams and mind-blasting prophecies they claim are sent by the gods themselves. These are not a certain guarantee of what is to pass, but instead potential futures that the Warqueen must bring about to maintain divine favour. When such a vision is received a Warqueen will muster the hundreds of warriors at her beck and call, leading them to ensure that the oaths she has sworn are fulfilled – no matter who, or what, stands in her way.

THE MANY GIFTS OF GODBLADE

The Ravagers are conquerors all, and their vast hordes have long been the bane of the Mortal Realms. The champions that lead their marauding armies maintain their position through dark charisma and brutal skill, but for those who court the favour of the Chaos Gods, death is far from the grimmest of ends…

Ozrakiah always feasted the night before a fight. Bloody porcine flesh, fruits dripping with sour juice, tribal ale thickened with strengthening gruel… His admirers kept him well-fed, knowing that each duel brought glory to them all. He was their banner. Their champion. He butchered the best and most blessed from rival tribes, and while his foes' warbands cursed his name, his own people hailed him as a legend.

But single combat drained a man in a way that war did not. War sapped the endurance, aye, no question, but open battle was a storm of chaos and sound and emotion. A duel, despite the cries of the crowd, was strangely silent. To go toe to toe with another warrior took patience, focus and self-control. Unrestrained wrath had its place in the shieldwall, where aggression and brute luck often overcame skill, but for a gladiator… No, naked rage was the recourse of desperate fools. Most often it ended up with them staring at the sky, throat-slit and gut-gashed, as their blood reddened the arena sands.

One of the first lessons Ozrakiah had learned was how well the carrion-hawks fed on the flesh of the angry and the careless. He saw it during his first days, took it to heart, and soon began teaching it to his rivals, delivering the lesson onward with the edges of his blades.

He took a deep swallow from his ivory drinking horn, washing down the bitterness of the ghura berries that still stained his lips black. Vile they might be, but they eased the blood's heat, preventing head pain in prolonged sunlight. They also thickened his spit, not enough to heighten his thirst, but enough that a mouthful of saliva spat onto his palms before a duel helped keep them dry of sweat. A good grip on your blades was yet another key to staying alive; Ozrakiah had seen more than one veteran meet death purely from being disarmed by a cunning opponent.

Tricks like this were what set him apart from many of his brother- and sister-gladiators. He had the strength, aye, but so many could lay claim to bare might. Ozrakiah coupled his strength with a sense of cautious cunning.

It was why he was rune-scarred with the gods' favour, his body infused with their blessings, and why all his rivals had gone to their funeral pyres.

'More ale!' he called out to the closest slave-girl. His dark eyes followed the sway of her slim hips as she moved to obey, and he flashed his teeth in a conqueror's smile.

It was good to be a legend.

The beast moans for more. More swill, more filth, more of the bones and offal and entrails that its masters hurl in its direction.

'Godblade hungers!' one of the beast's jailers calls out, inciting a chorus of jeers.

The beast looks up at the laughter, its myriad eyes glaring bloodshot and proud from seven separate faces. Seven fanged maws drawl a wordless oath of righteous hate, each out of time and tune with the others. Claws – many, many claws – close and open and tense and curl.

The chains binding the beast to the stone pillar aren't enough; several of its masters keep their spears levelled at the creature, especially during its feeding hours.

In the past, the shamans told their barbaric brethren that the monster possesses nothing as clear as thought. Instinct drives it in place of intelligence, and where there should be comprehension, there is only emotion. It hungers, it hurts, it kills, it feeds. It is a thing made of desires so crude and fierce they eclipse all possible human savagery.

It moans from its many mouths now, a starvation growl.

A sacrifice is brought forth, driven forward by those same spears. The captive protests as they always do – insisting her crimes were nothing, that she's innocent of the sins that have already damned her. Her captors know she's a thief and a murderess, and this would be her fate even if those weren't the least of her crimes. She swears she'll be of use in the battle tomorrow, but that's the saddest jest of all: the Raven's Cry Clan hardly needs the dubious allegiance of a single lying murderer. Their victory will be earned with iron and honour, blood and glory. Not the mewling of prisoners too weak to get away with their crimes.

They cast her into the pit, followed by the sound of cheering from a thousand throats.

There's a fight, just like there always is; and just like always, it's over in moments.

The murderess falls silent.

And Godblade feeds.

The battle begins at dawn the next day, signalled by the rising sun. The clans' war-horns cut the lightening sky with their droning calls, and thunder rings out across the land. Not, this time, the hollow thunder of Sigmar's arcane storms, but a far sweeter, far holier sound: the tectonic tread of a thousand tribes. A million axe-wielders and sword-killers, led by their champions, charging beneath the banners of their gods.

Godblade fights at the battle's very heart. The creature is a storm of twisted talons that grasp and sever and slice. It enters the city with the first wave, scrabbling over the ruined marble walls, shrieking at the defenders too brave or too foolish to run.

Around its colossal form, the horde charges, drowning out all other sound with their war cries. So many of them, not a tide of sweating, stinking humanity, but an ocean of them, flooding through the streets of the breached city.

Angels with wings of searing light fall from the sky, brought down by javelin casts and twisted, smoky magic. Godblade slaughters several of the barbarians nearby in a frenzy of need, throwing them from the downed form of one of Sigmar's winged sons. The beast delimbs the Stormcast with the same mindless ease of a child taking apart an insect. It tries to devour the remains, but ends up only with bloody, fire-blackened maw, scorched by lightning.

They have no blood to drink. No meat to eat. This just drives the creature to fresh heights of frustrated rage.

The battle ends as the city burns. Great icons are raised from the bodies of the slain, chained together to form sacred symbols. Slave-caravans take shape at the behest of leering barbarians.

Godblade stands in a plaza of broken marble, aching, starving, bellowing.

'Yoke the spawn!' the tribesmen are crying, laughing, yelling. They laugh even as their own kinsmen die in Godblade's claws. It's a game now: a savage game, where glory is earned in being one of those who manages to chain the beast down.

Even bound, Godblade rages. It lashes out with claws that can't reach its tormentors. It tries to chew through its chains, breaking its teeth, only for them to regrow each dawn. It bashes itself against the stone pillar, leaving smears of something that isn't quite blood.

Eventually, pacified by shamanic sorcery and drugged meat, the beast finally crawls into a fitful sleep. It twitches in its slumber the way true animals do, though its captors know this is nothing more than the tensing of muscle answering flashes of tainted emotion.

Chaos Spawn cannot think. They cannot remember who they once were.

Everyone knows this.

And so, surely, Godblade cannot dream.

Ozrakiah dragged his forearm across his brow, banishing the sweat before it could drip into his eyes. The crowd's baying and roaring presses at his senses, somehow tidal, inevitable. It's as familiar to him as the feel of his axes in his hands, and as welcome as the sunlight on his bare, rune-scarred skin.

The arena was an unkind mistress at times, generous only with the scars she gave. But the gods? They rewarded those that performed for their pleasure. Ozrakiah wasn't a man that believed in hiding his god-granted gifts, and proudly he displayed the changes wrought upon him by the pantheon. The crescent spikes that crested out from his spine. The daggers of bone protruding from his elbows. The thickening of his flesh to something like lizard-leather, patches of darkened beasthide capable of breaking careless blades.

He towered above his foes. All of them. The sheer physicality he was capable of left pride forever whispering at the edge of his senses: an undercurrent to every breath he drew in, and to each beat of his heart.

Ozrakiah stepped over the body of the last fool he downed, and played to the watching tribespeople, raising his blades and clashing them together in the high sun. Blood flecked his face as it spattered from the crashing steel. The clansmen roared their acclaim.

Another tribe sent a man forward, this one snake-lean and wielding a half-pike. Ozrakiah scented the salty lizard-mucus coating the speartip, and he saw where it glistened in the midday heat.

Another wretch with a poisoned blade, then. So be it.

Ozrakiah spat into the sand, showing just what he thought of his opponent's chances.

'Do you hear them?' he asked the advancing tribesman. He even held his arms to the side, aiming both axes at the crowd, making his point with a flourish. 'Do you hear our people baying for your blood?'

The newcomer's reply was irrelevant. Ozrakiah paid it no mind at all. He let the doomed man speak his piece, then advanced with his axes held low, as thousands of watching warriors read the familiar oath on his moving lips.

'I am Ozrakiah Godblade of the Raven's Cry Clan, and I pledge your death to the pantheon.'

This fool would die, and then the next, and the next, and any that dared follow.

What gifts, what blessings, would the gods grant him next?

How high might he one day rise?

MASTERS OF CHAOS MAGIC

In their quest for unlimited power, sorcerers bargain with daemons and perform unspeakable acts of evil. Whether they are tribal shamans leading rituals to please their atavistic gods, or sinister Cabalists willing to pay any price for the knowledge they seek, these warlocks are amongst the most formidable Slaves to Darkness.

CHAOS SORCERER LORDS

With but a single incantation, a Sorcerer Lord summons the dark magics of Chaos to flense a man's soul or infuse his limbs with daemonic power. Such spellcraft comes naturally to these champions, for they are the warlocks and shamans of the Slaves to Darkness. They have a natural affinity with the wild energies of Chaos, and can shape the power of magic as they desire; such potential always come with a price, however. The ease with which a sorcerer commands arcane energies gives them none of the respect for this deadly tool that is bequeathed to more traditional mages. As they recklessly employ dark magic to achieve their sinister goals, they inevitably slip deeper into madness and mutation.

Sorcerer Lords are the oracles and seers of the Slaves to Darkness, and as such hold a particularly vital position amongst the dark tribes. It is they who have the most direct connection to the Chaos Gods, save in the case of the almighty Daemon Princes, and as such it is they who can best divine how a warrior or warband may gain glory in the eyes of their patron. It is considered a poor omen in many tribes to slay a sorcerer, though this will not stop an aspirant champion from making the attempt should they believe that the gods demand it. Of course, Sorcerer Lords are more than capable of defending themselves. Not only are they able to hurl bolts of killing energy or twist a foe's body into new and unsettling form, but many sorcerers – especially those who have sworn themselves, knowingly or otherwise, to Tzeentch – possess a measure of foresight that allows them to often presage and account for impending betrayals. Only those who lose the favour of the gods discover that their oracular visions prove lacking or even deliberately misleading; as such, Sorcerer Lords tend to be amongst the most depraved Slaves to Darkness, for to maintain their divine protection they will willingly and joyously commit any act, no matter how vile.

Most Hordes include several sorcerers amongst their number. Though they often act as viziers to an Overlord of more martial leaning, a Sorcerer Lord can also claim dominion of the Horde entire. This is particularly true in the case of the Cabalists, whose armies are akin to a coven of warlocks surrounded by superstitious pawns and favoured enforcers, forever hunting new sources of arcane power. It is also the sorcerers of a Horde who lead the rituals to please the gods. These rites take many forms, and the only thing that unites them is their disregard for natural law or common decency. Only those who worship the Lord of War above all others do not partake in these rituals, for they honour the gods primarily through the shedding of blood, and in the vast majority of cases have utter contempt for sorcery. It takes a particularly powerful Overlord to compel these war-worshippers to tolerate a sorcerer's presence, and they are not always successful. The Doomskull Horde, once the scourge of the underworld of Athanasia, was violently partitioned when the worshippers of the Crimson Grave – a patron of violent death with many followers throughout the Horde – rebelled against the sorcerer coven they believed was manipulating their Overlord. Battle still rages across the plains of the underworld to this day, the magical prowess of the Sorcerer Lords allowing them to hold their own against many times their number of foes.

Owing to their skill in, and occasional reliance on, the power of magic, sorcerers are rarely as physically imposing as the Chaos Lords. Some seek to redress this

THE GAUNT SUMMONERS

Nine is the number of the Gaunt Summoners, those strange daemon-sorcerers of Tzeentch that serve the will of the Everchosen. From the eldritch fortresses known as the Silver Towers, these duplicitous creatures plot a web of manipulation that spans entire realms. It was only through great guile that Archaon bound the Summoners to his will, gaining knowledge of each daemon's true name before working a subtle sorcery to trap them in a prison of their own doubts and horror. The Everchosen soon put his powerful new servants to work, unleashing their sorceries on hundreds of battlefields and harnessing their talents for misdirection to affect many more.

Gaunt Summoners often patronise Arcanites cults, or otherwise conspire with fellow Tzeentchian daemons, for they rail at their servitude and seek always to elude Archaon's clutches. When the Everchosen calls, however, they must answer. Hovering above the battlefield on Discs of Tzeentch, Gaunt Summoners unleash torrents of witchfire, or split the skin of reality to call forth the daemons of the Dark Gods. The names of these beings have passed into infamy. The Watcher King, the Tyrant of Eyes, Stilskeen: each serves Archaon in their own way, and when they fight alongside their lords of Chaos, there are few who can stand against their magical onslaught and immortal cunning.

balance through enslaving a fearsome Manticore to their will. Unlike Chaos Lords, sorcerers employ spells of binding and mental domination to enthral these primal beasts and force them to submit. More than one warlock has discovered the peril of attempting to force servitude on a Manticore, especially should their magical control slip. Yet those who manage to successfully bind such a creature find themselves with a mount that responds almost instantly to their every whim, furiously savaging the foe while the Sorcerer Lord is free to work their foul magic unimpeded.

THE GODSWORN HUNT

The Black Fang are one of the countless tribes that, over the centuries, have pledged themselves to the Gods of Chaos. None amongst their number are more infamous than the shaman Theddra Skull-Scryer and the warband known as the Godsworn Hunt. All these warriors consider themselves to be Darkoath, swearing great pacts to the dark pantheon in return for reward. Yet the oath made by the Godsworn Hunt is particularly ambitious: they have sworn the Pact of Soul and Iron, offering the lives of Sigmar's Stormcast Eternals in sacrifice to the gods.

In order to make good this pact, Theddra has led the Godsworn Hunt into the depths of Shadespire – though on occasion she is able to escape its boundaries for a time to fight alongside the Hordes of the Slaves to Darkness. Skull-Scryer's command of magic is powerful and instinctive, and those assailed by her sorceries find their bodies become withered and emaciated as all vitality is drained from them. Such enforced weakness makes them easy prey for the remainder of the Godsworn Hunt. Whether they are cut down by the heavy blades of Grundann Blood-Eye and Shond Head-Claimer, spitted by Jagathra's javelin, stuck with arrows by the dead-eyed Ollo, or savaged by the slavering hound known as Grawl, the foes of the Godsworn Hunt soon meet grisly ends – their lives offered in tribute to the great gods beyond.

MAGIC OF THE DARK GODS

The magic wielded by the shamans of the dark tribes involves channelling the raw power of Chaos. This is a perilous affair, for mortals were never supposed to touch the essence of the gods and survive. Over the centuries, sorcerers have deduced ways to mitigate the damaging effects of Chaos magic without diminishing its potency; ritual sacrifice to appease the gods' soul-hunger is common, particularly amongst the Cabalist covens. Pacts with daemonic entities are also commonplace, though many sorcerers discover in the end that their otherworldly patron does not have their best interests in mind.

Since the dawning of the Arcanum Optimar, sorcerers have been able to fashion lingering manifestations of magic. The pantheistic worship of most tribes means that these spells draw upon Chaos in all its glory, though their form can differ based on the devotion of the caster. Eightfold Doom-Sigils burn in the skies above the greatest slaughters, drawing the souls of the slain unto them and empowering the servants of the gods. Realmscourge Ruptures surge forth as a manifestation of the tortured land, impaling all in their path. Most terrible are the Darkfire Daemonrifts, for these are gateways to the Realm of Chaos itself, cracks in reality that split the sky and from which daemonic predators unleash concentrated gouts of warping Chaotic essence.

THE WEIGHT OF SACRIFICE

Blood-mages and dark-hearted seers, the Cabalists exchange the lives of their followers for greater command of the arcane. These fell sorcerers possess vast eldritch might, but always they must contend with the soul-hunger of the gods – for those voracious beings demand ever higher prices from their supplicants.

When the tribe spoke of Arjah, they hailed his victories. They boasted of his wisdom, his insight, his feats of sorcery. Above all, they praised him for the acuity of his prophecy. Who else could read What Would Be in the random ripples of a knife stroked through a blood pool? Who else could perceive the skeins of Fate by clawing through the labyrinth of an animal's guts?

For generations he'd served as God-speaker to a succession of Warchiefs and Warqueens, counselling them when they beseeched him, wielding his magic in war when they required it, and betraying them to their deaths when he believed the tribe would thrive under a new leader.

Since the realms had cracked open and disgorged the grave-stinking taint of the Death God's whisperings, that chilling stench had woven its way into many of his conjurings. With lip-curling irritation, Arjah began to take a more active guiding hand in his clan's battles. Less often did they shed blood over land or mere pride; more and more often he bid the clanlords remember that there were other avenues to glory. He poured promises of power into their ears, drip by murmured drip, telling them of ancient tombs now broken open to the light, and the artefacts that lay, untouched for millennia, within.

Blades from forgotten empires, stained with ancient magic, soon found their way into his warriors' hands. Trinkets and curios containing long-lost arcane weavings found their way into his care, while the weaker talismans were given as gifts to his acolytes.

And what of the great and terrible spells now tearing their way across the land? The tempests of shrieking flame, the groundquakes that devoured warriors with maws of stone, the jagged mirrors that hissed each of a man's sins… Arjah had faced them himself, bloody hands raised, his cracking voice lifted to sing the pantheon's praises, and he'd turned these fragments of malignant energy to his own desires.

They could not be bound, not reliably, no. But they could be unleashed.

All of these deeds only added to the respect he was offered, of course. He deserved nothing less. As he grew in power, so did his tribe. No soul had served his people as well as Arjah himself.

He had lived now for almost three hundred years. How close was he to what he desired? How far from it, yet?

Apotheosis. Ascension. Immortality. He was close. He had to be.

This is how his tribe spoke of him to his face; how they boasted of him to warriors of other clans.

But when they whispered amongst themselves away from the night-fires, they spoke most often of his failure.

His one failure.

Arjah suspected he wouldn't survive another such cataclysm. Even if he lived through the unleashing of magics, which was by no means assured, the tribe would likely take his head in the belief the gods had abandoned him.

And… would they be wrong to do so?

Perhaps. Perhaps not.

On the night of his failure, the arcane backlash had raked his flesh with fire, stealing an eye, an ear, and scalding his left arm into a tarnished thing of burn scars and aching bone. Worst of all was the mangled ruin of his left leg, leaving him with a limp that he'd endure until his dying day.

A day that might, if the omens continued as they were, already be at hand.

It wasn't supposed to be this way. He'd done everything right the first time. Hadn't he? Had he not done all that the gods demanded of him? Had he not prepared everything to perfection, all in accordance with the desires of the divine?

Sacrifice. That was the fulcrum upon which the gods' favour balanced. Every hedge witch and dabbler knew it, but understanding it could be the work of a lifetime. What mortal mind could really attune itself to the twisted web of a god's desires? Every spell was a leap of faith. Every ritual was hope and belief wrapped in tangled prayer.

Too many brutes believed sacrifice was nothing more than cutting the hearts from a few captives and raising that blood-soaked harvest to the sky. Where was the sacrifice in such a deed? Such blood-rites were offerings, not sacrifices, for nothing of true value was freely given. The sorcerer suffered no loss. How then would the gods ever care for such spiritually thin pledges of devotion?

Arjah had thought long and hard over this, as his weeping wounds cooled to scars.

Tomorrow would be a time of testing. He could walk again, albeit haltingly, and he was ready to avenge his failure.

The last time, somehow the sacrifice had been unworthy. The skull of his father, a haunted relic steeped in sanguine energies; he had crushed it to dust for the sake of a spell reagent. His own wife, a crone now but still dear to him, had died for his sake, cut open by his ritual knife so her blood would add another ingredient to the spellweaving.

Three of his apprentices, the three most promising of his tribe's young hexweavers; each one was held down by warriors at Arjah's command and beheaded with the Warqueen's axe. And as if this were not enough, he'd cast aside a dozen artefacts and talismans of great use to the tribe, each one plundered at great cost in life from the tombs of fallen kingdoms, sacrificed for the sake of this one arcane weaving.

And it hadn't been enough. The backlash had almost killed him, and in his fevered dreams on the edge of death, he'd heard the gods' laughter. If he heard that sound again, he feared it would forever drive all reason from his skull.

Arjah summoned his son for the final preparations, and the young man attended him in his animal-hide tent, crouching before the brazier. Arjah watched him brush desert dust from his boots, so as not to dirty the fur rugs. The boy had manners.

His son, Nagarah, was cast in his image: thin, hook-nosed, draped in beast-furs and amulets of jade and bone. He was a God-speaker like his father. The tribe's last God-speaker. The future of the clan.

Arjah could understand the weight of that burden all too well, for everything he'd done across the centuries of his life had been for the clan. So he'd told himself, decade after decade, and so he'd proved through countless deeds.

'The clan lives or dies with you, Nagarah. I read that truth in the bowel-ropes of a Gryph-hound, with no sign of disease in the intestinal meat. The soothsaying was pure, with no chance of flaw. Hear me when I say this. No matter what happens to me, the clan lives or dies with you.'

Arjah needed to say no more. The younger man nodded, for he'd read the same fate in his own prophecies.

'I will carry your teachings forward.'

'Yes. You have learned well, son.'

Arjah drew his sacrificial kris, the bone handle worn smooth after two centuries of use, the blade slender, ever sharp, jagged to promote blood flow. He turned it in his hand, letting the firelight play over the polished human-ivory.

'Why do you weep, Father?'

'Because there is one final lesson,' Arjah said softly. 'A lesson in meaningful sacrifice.'

Dawn came, and the battle came with it.

For Arjah, standing far from the crash of blooded iron and the thunder of splintering shields, the fighting was naught but a distraction. He was alone atop a small rise, facing his rivals across the desert's sweeping dunes. Five of them opposed him; five aelven sorcerers armed with armour of spell-shaped metal, bearing mother-of-pearl blades. The air shimmered around them with impossible mirages: vast sailing ships gone to rot and ruin; kingdoms of coral spires that couldn't exist.

Arjah knew nothing of their culture. He cared nothing, either. The battle raged as battles do; the sorcerers cared only for their own efforts.

The spells they duelled over were Endless, each one a volatile phantasm first vomited up by the Death God's torture of the Mortal Realms, now unchained and destructive beyond measure. Arjah had bound several of them – perhaps 'contained' was a better term – within his last remaining artefacts, knowing these were temporary cages at best. At the battle's apex, he shattered the brass figurines restraining the elemental sorceries, and an eruption of fanged light and spectral wrath burst forth across the desert.

His rivals responded in kind, just as Arjah had foreseen. The battlefield rang with the cacophonous displays of their own Endless revelations. Within minutes, both armies warred in scattered conclaves, the battle dissolving into disorder. Sorcery gouged chasms through the desert, sucking the sandy ground from beneath warriors' feet. Men and aelves ignited with unquenchable flame. Blades manifested from nowhere, whirling into dances at the behest of distant magicians, carving agony across the bodies of those nearby.

He felt the aelven mages wresting control of his magic away from him, bending the brutal conjurings to their own wills, reshaping them as they did so. The ghostly jaws of a great Manticore became something more sharklike, a maw lined with rows of knife-teeth instead of great crescent-fangs. Its blazing form churned red as it tore through the warriors of Arjah's clan. One by one, spell by spell, the aelves re-wove the unleashed magic, turning it upon the human horde. God-banners went up in flames as their bearers burned.

Even one-eyed, one-eared, one-armed, the sorcerer could resist and repel the aelves' efforts. The gods were watching, they were with him, and he felt their attentions running through his veins with each beat of his heart. With them as his witness, he would be stronger than ever. He could save his clan and win the war.

Sacrifice.

Apotheosis. Ascension. Immortality.

Arjah drew his ritual knife and added his will to that of his foes. The spells devouring his kin surged with renewed force, the fires searing even fiercer, the blades peeling flesh from bone. He could hear his tribe crying for him on the rising wind, wailing for his aid, none of them aware that every one of their ignorant screams was a prayer.

Something unfolded in the meat of his mind: a sound that wasn't a sound, a sensation that wasn't a feeling. A presence. Laughter? Was it laughter? Had he failed again?

No. Not laughter. Something else.

The God-speaker held his kris, still red with his son's dried blood, and stood alone at the battlefield's edge, watching his people die.

'Is this enough?' he screamed into the wind. 'IS THIS ENOUGH!?'

He did not have to wait long for an answer.

THE LOST AND THE DAMNED

Among the Slaves to Darkness are those who feel the pull of the gods stronger than most. From the vast legions of Chaos Warriors fighting in the armies of the Ravagers, to elite bands of Chosen serving the will of the Daemon Princes of the Despoilers, these darkly blessed warriors will never rest in their desire to see civilisation toppled.

CHAOS WARRIORS

When a member of the dark tribes becomes a Chaos Warrior, they leave behind all comforts of hearth and family. For them, only a lifetime of war awaits. Such is the will of the gods, for it is through becoming a Chaos Warrior that a mortal takes their first true step upon the Path to Glory. It is a decision from which there is almost no returning, for the dark pantheon are jealous beings, and they have little patience for mortal doubt or regret.

Chaos Warriors are formidable fighters, easily a match for Sigmar's Stormcast Eternals. The armour they wear is thick and strong, marked with runes of the dark tongue to bolster the wearer's stamina and ward off enemy blows. Their weapons, typically wicked blades or crushing maces, can rend flesh and crush bone with a single blow; some tribes forge their own weapons, whereas others rely on the services of fallen duardin smiths to supply their need for armaments, though in all cases new-forged blades of the Slaves to Darkness are typically cooled in fresh lifeblood. Yet for all these deadly tools of war, it is the Chaos Warriors themselves that are the most fearsome proposition for their enemies. The quest for glory has seen them test their skills in countless conflicts, their physiques strengthened by the gifts of their gods and their battle instincts honed to a terrifying edge.

Beneath ragged banners depicting the sigils of the dark pantheon, warbands of Chaos Warriors form the armoured fist of many Hordes. Though typically outnumbered by the barbarous Marauders, the sheer expanse of the realms ensures that there is almost always a steady supply of these ironclad warriors willing to swear their allegiance to a powerful champion or Overlord. Some warbands, or even Hordes, are comprised almost entirely of Chaos Warriors, particularly those who seek closer communion with the Ruinous Powers and are on their way to becoming one of the Godtouched. Typically, Chaos Warriors make common cause with those who worship the same, or at least similar, interpretations of one or all of the Ruinous Powers. On occasion an entire tribe may declare themselves upon the Path to Glory and become Chaos Warriors at the same time, though this is rare; in most cases warbands of Chaos Warriors will not necessarily hail from the same tribe as a Horde's Godsworn Overlord. However they assemble, Chaos Warriors fight as a grinding legion of steel and fury, using their skill at arms and formidable numbers to crush all beneath them.

Leading each warband of Chaos Warriors will be an Aspiring Champion. Though they have not yet caught the gaze of the gods proper, this warrior has proven themselves sufficiently worthy to claim the honour of leading their kin to war. An Aspiring Champion must be forever wary of rivals from within their own warband, for few of the gods worshipped by the Slaves to Darkness see any issue with

treachery. Should they successfully maintain their position however, an Aspiring Champion will no doubt begin to accrue their own personal saga of fell deeds, and in time will rise to higher ranks of champion – perhaps one day even becoming a Godsworn Overlord themselves.

CHOSEN

Should a Chaos Warrior please the gods and survive the constant battles they must fight, they may eventually become one of the Chosen. They are held in awe by their fellow Slaves to Darkness. Whether through attracting daemons to grant them favour, completing great quests in the name of their patron, or simply wreaking unimaginable carnage across the Mortal Realms, each Chosen stands as an exemplar amongst the armies of Chaos. Wielding cursed Soul-splitter blades, heavy two-handed axes with the power to sever a foe's animus from their body, they stride at the head of the armies of darkness, eager to lay waste to the enemies of the gods.

Chosen warbands are amongst the most deadly elements of a Horde, and are often limited in number – though many Despoiler Hordes contain considerable numbers of these exalted warriors, the better to serve the ruling Daemon Prince's will. Typically, they take to the field wherever the fighting is thickest. This is not purely to leverage their own formidable skills, though certainly there are few beings in all the realms that can stand before these elite warriors and hope to survive, let alone triumph. Other Slaves to Darkness are intensely inspired by the sheer, ruinous violence dealt out by these favoured warbands. As the Chosen slaughter the foe, those servants of Chaos around them fight all the harder, each seeking to draw similar godly attention onto themselves. Under the leadership of the Exalted Champions – warriors who are only a step away from having several warbands under their command – the Chosen fearlessly enter battle against any foe, axes swinging in great crimson arcs as they howl praise to the watching gods.

CHAOS KNIGHTS

To become a Chaos Knight, a Slave to Darkness must typically have walked the ruinous path for many years. Their armour – whether forged from Chamonite steel, corrupted ironoak, or stranger materials besides – has twisted to become jagged and brutal, and from the visors of their helmets glows an eerie light that burns with dark power. Mutations wrack their bodies, and the ensorcelled weapons they take to battle are a match for any Sigmarite blade. Even the steeds they ride are not free from the touch of the Ruinous Powers; these dark chargers are hulking muscular beasts whose breath is like cinder, and who are every bit as fierce as their riders. To tame such a beast requires a warrior of singular strength and focus, but on rare occasions entire knightly orders will slip into the grasp of Chaos, their faithful mounts being remade just as the warriors themselves are.

Chaos Knights are amongst the most feared Slaves to Darkness. Though some consider themselves noble or chivalric in their own, infernal fashion, in truth they are butchers and madmen consumed by their endless quest for glory. So proud are they that they shall dip their banner for none save the Godsworn Overlord of their Horde, or otherwise the Everchosen himself. When they hit the enemy line it is as if the gods themselves have given their murderous fury physical, iron-hard form. Just as deadly as the skill of the Chaos Knights is the terrifying reputation their slaughters have garnered. Few foes have not heard tell of some atrocity perpetuated by warbands of these black-hearted killers, and as the Chaos Knights close – lances levelled and foul war cries on their lips – many consider it better to take their chances by fleeing rather than trying to withstand the charge of these merciless champions.

CHARIOTEERS OF CHAOS

Many Slaves to Darkness tribes dwell upon the plains of the Mortal Realms, where the acts of barbarism and savagery needed to survive made it easy for the Gods of Chaos to pervert their ancestral customs and beliefs. This reality ensures that chariots have always been a common sight amongst the Hordes. These mobile fighting platforms are well suited for warfare upon the open vistas of the realms, allowing a warrior to cross great distances at speed without growing tired – as well as using the mass of the chariot itself as a brutally effective weapon.

Most Chaos Chariots are pulled by a pair of muscular steeds. As the beasts snort and whinny, fury pounding through their minds, they charge forth under the lash of their driver to close with the enemy. Some armies use chariots as steady platforms from which to fire projectiles, but such cowardice has no place amongst the Slaves to Darkness. Instead, Chaos Chariots will smash straight into – and often through – the enemy lines, crushing the foe beneath their grinding wheels as the charioteers set about them with long-hafted axes and flails. Often several chariots will operate in concert to punch a hole through the enemy's defences, led by a skilled Exalted Charioteer who has fought for many years from the back of his trusty war machine. The solid construction of a Chaos Chariot's frame renders it highly resilient, easily able to withstand the blows of the enemy as it wheels around for another pass.

On occasion, a tribe may capture a brutish creature known as a Gorebeast to pull one of their chariots. Little is known of these scaly monstrosities, save that they can be found across the realms wherever the touch of Chaos lingers, and that they possess a monstrous strength. Binding a Gorebeast is no easy feat, and only the most physically imposing charioteers can hope to force such a monster to submit. The natural inclination for destruction these creatures possess does, however, make them highly effective weapons; once hitched to a chariot a Gorebeast will likely charge the first enemy that it sees, its sheer bulk and heavy fists wreaking untold havoc as the charioteer themselves simply tries to keep pace with the creature's spiralling kill-count.

WARRIORS OF THE BLASTED WASTES

The warriors of the dark tribes are known as Marauders. Though they have yet to catch the notice of the gods, these barbarians are deadly fighters, hardened by life under the grip of Chaos. Marching alongside strange shrines and the savage beasts of the wastes, these ferocious fighters honour their gods with every life they take.

MARAUDERS

From lands suffused with the corrupting touch of Chaos come the Marauder tribes. Numbering in the hundreds of thousands, these barbarous Chaos worshippers fight in the name of the Ruinous Powers and for the simple joy of battle alike. Though they are mere mortals, and individually no match for the monsters and demigods that walk the realms, when they fight in great numbers and harness the dark blessings of the Chaos Gods, they are more than capable of sweeping away all before them in a frenzy of battle-lust.

While Marauders have not yet made the ultimate surrender to the gods that sees them reborn in the form of a Chaos Warrior, a life of constant battle amidst the Dominion of Chaos still renders them naturally talented fighters; they must be, for those too weak to defend themselves soon become prey. Their tribal communities may be considered primitive by those sneering Azyrites who dwell far from the Marauders' blades, but they are strong and robust, well suited for life amidst the hard wilds of the realms. These tribes can vary wildly in size, from a handful of Marauders

under a charismatic chieftain to vast throngs of barbarians united by a particular shaman or, with increasing regularity, a warleader of the Darkoath. It is unusual – though far from unheard of – for a Marauder tribe to dedicate all its worship towards a single god. Their tribal customs often push them into venerating several deities, and they will pray to different aspects of Chaos as and when they see fit. In larger tribes, those who do gravitate towards a certain patron will form like-minded warbands, often taking to battle under a similarly devoted champion. These Marauders tend to be considered outsiders amongst most tribes, though in the case of the Godtouched such furious zealots are the norm.

Marauders need little encouragement to join the Horde of a Godsworn Overlord; should the tribe's oracles claim it to be the gods' will, warband after warband will march forth to spread death and carnage. Often, these battles will be fought against rival followers of Chaos, hordes and warbands clashing to prove the superiority of their gods and their Overlord. Defeat in such a battle does not necessarily mean death for a Marauder, however. Those who fight with courage and skill will be absorbed into the ranks of the triumphant Horde, either forming new warbands of their fellow survivors or joining battle-proven groups of Marauders who match their temperament.

When the Slaves to Darkness wage war against the civilised lands, it is Marauders who make up much of a Horde's strength – especially in the vast legions of the Ravagers. Though many of them may fall to the spells and firepower of their more civilised enemies, those who suffer the bite of the barbarians' axes soon learn to fear them, and should a Marauder excel under the gaze of the gods, the Path to Glory may await them yet.

MARAUDER HORSEMEN

Marauder Horsemen pride themselves on being the first warriors of the Horde to sink their blades into the flesh of the enemy. Many Slaves to Darkness tribes have an affinity with equine creatures, for the hardy beasts are perfect for crossing vast wildernesses at speed or running down fleeing prey. Ownership of such a beast is often considered a mark of status and favour, and some warbands – or in rarer cases whole tribes – take this horse-mastery to new levels, becoming amongst the most feared light cavalry in the realms. Mounted upon their trusty steeds, beasts bred more for speed and endurance than the raw strength of a Chaos Knight's mount, they thunder across the battlefield, kicking up great clouds of dust behind them to herald their coming before joyously plunging into the thick of melee.

Marauder Horsemen are some of the few Slaves to Darkness who bring missile weaponry to battle, in the form of stout javelins. Every wise Champion knows the advantages to having a force of predatory outriders who can engage the foe from a distance and provide time for the rest of the Horde to advance, as well as ride down those who impotently attempt to flee. Horsemen warbands tend to worship the Chaos Powers as bloodthirsty hunter-lords, winged seraphim of inevitable death, and preening deities of the perfect kill. The rituals to please these beings commonly revolve around celebrating the moment death is delivered, and often a Horseman's steed joins the rite by trampling a captive under iron-shod hooves. Though Marauder Horsemen are masters of the feigned flight and hit-and-run attack, their devotion to the gods cannot be denied. When battle is joined they will charge into the fray as eagerly as any of their fellow warbands, howling praises and oaths as they ride down non-believers.

WARSHRINES

Carried into battle by mutant abominations captured from across the twisted landscapes of the realms – or, on occasion, created from members of a tribe who displeased the local shaman – Warshrines are physical testaments to the power of the Chaos Gods. Dark flames flicker in braziers mounted across the shrine's platform, while daemonic faces wrought in bronze or stranger materials leer across its flanks. Above the blood-slicked altar itself is mounted a grand sigil of the eight-pointed star. It is through this portal that the energies of the Realm of Chaos are channelled by the Warshrine's keeper. Whether it is ordained with the symbol of one of the Ruinous Powers – common in Godtouched warbands – or left as an icon of unaligned Chaos in all its majesty, warriors of the Slaves to Darkness rally to a Warshrine as a symbol of their god's supremacy.

As the Shrinemaster leads all manner of dark rituals, the baroque construction of the Warshrine acts as a lodestone for the raw energies of Chaos. The runes surrounding the great sigil glow with an unearthly light, offering a measure of divine protection to those of the devoted who cluster in its presence. When the Shrinemaster utters the blackest of invocations, however, the true might of the gods is made manifest. Even those who do not favour the patron to which the Warshrine is dedicated are likely to receive a portion of the divine power flowing from it; those who do venerate the Shrinekeeper's deity above all become orders of magnitude more deadly still, their dedication rewarded by their chosen god.

FURIES

Furies are spiteful daemons who swarm throughout the Chaos-tainted lands of the realms in great number. Though they are minor daemonic entities compared to the creatures in the legions of the Dark Gods within the Realm of Chaos, their predatory instincts and natural cunning makes them vicious predators. Those who have journeyed into the domains of Chaos – particularly the warbands who fight in the lands of the Eightpoints – have learned to dread the chorus of beating, leathery wings that heralds the arrival of a Fury pack.

Furies are not aligned with any of the Dark Gods – rather, they are embodiments of the raw stuff of Chaos, sentient shards of pure malice that follow the armies of the Slaves to Darkness out of a base urge to maim and kill. As such, Furies are particularly self-serving even by the standards of daemons, forever seeking ways to improve their lot and cast down their rivals. They can be cajoled, bound or bargained with by a Champion of Chaos to join their warbands in battle, where the Furies' propensity for attacking swiftly and preying upon the weak makes them the terror of isolated enemies. Should a flock of Furies think that the fight is going against them, they are swift to pull out of harm's way – though will always return when the enemy's back is turned, hungry for vengeance.

RAPTORYX

Raptoryx are ferocious avian creatures that swarm across the Eightpoints in search of prey. Each has many eyes, a broad, hooked beak and a viciously spiked tail, though as with all things touched by the gods there is only scant commonality between them. They were once natural forms of wildlife, but over the centuries the taint of Chaos has seen them twisted into a menacing new form. Some have passed through the great gates of the Eightpoints to spread across the Mortal Realms beyond, and the number of lands that have not echoed to the shrieks of a Raptoryx flock grows smaller every day.

Raptoryx can never be truly tamed; their primitive minds are too consumed with bestial fury to accept any kind of captivity. They can, however, be directed against a particular enemy by skilled beastmasters. Raptoryx possess a low cunning, and in sufficient numbers can savage prey many times their size. Those who underestimate the creatures soon learn their mistake, for the beasts' razor-sharp beaks are capable of bisecting a man with a single snapping bite, and they must be almost entirely hacked apart before succumbing to death's embrace.

THE DAEMONIC AND THE MONSTROUS

Stranger beings than mere mortals march in the armies of the Dark Gods. Lumbering alongside them are all manner of foul and terrifying beasts, twisted through the power of Chaos. Greatest of these are the Daemon Princes, those champions who have reached the apex of the Path to Glory, and been reborn as avatars of ruin.

BE'LAKOR

Be'lakor, the First Prince of Chaos, is an aberration. Alone amongst the Daemon Princes he ascended through the favour of all the dark pantheon. This level of relative autonomy makes Be'lakor particularly terrifying. His schemes straddle realms and span centuries, and though he has been observed fighting alongside the forces of all the Chaos Gods, his true goals remain unknown.

Many legends exist concerning Be'lakor's origins. Some believe that he was the first mortal to achieve apotheosis, but that as the gods raised up more of their servants to daemonhood, their first-born grew resentful – desiring to one day supplant the Dark Powers themselves. Another legend claims that Be'lakor sought to become the most favoured of champions. The gods were amused by his ambitions and cursed him to instead crown the Everchosen, sparking a mutual antipathy with Archaon. Across Ulgu can be found ancient pictograms depicting a being resembling Be'lakor, fuelling belief that he may once have been the ruler of the Grey Realm before the coming of Malerion, and that in his desire to maintain his throne against the aelven god he turned to the Dark Powers. Whatever the truth, Be'lakor remains a being of shadow and terror. His manipulations are subtle and far-ranging; when Be'lakor takes to battle his enemies find themselves playing perfectly into his hands, their horror at such sudden reversals fuelling the ancient daemon's hunger as he carves them apart.

DAEMON PRINCES

Few champions prove themselves worthy enough to ascend to daemonhood. It is not enough to be merely a talented warrior; as they walk the Path to Glory, a champion must perform countless heinous acts

that especially resonate with and empower their patron. Rarely are these deeds simple to accomplish, and so those who realise their ambitions and are reborn as Daemon Princes are amongst the deadliest beings in the realms.

While greater daemons may treat Daemon Princes with contempt – considering them tainted by their mortal origins – the Slaves to Darkness venerate these beings as proof of the reward for their devotion. Any who witness a Daemon Prince in battle can understand why a man might pledge themselves to the Dark Gods,

for the sheer physical might of a Daemon Prince matched with the hellish powers they can call upon can swiftly overwhelm even the greatest foes.

Though Daemon Princes are born of the Chaos Gods, and as such know much of their true nature, these beings rarely see any reason to dissuade tribes of the Slaves to Darkness from their existing beliefs – especially since the idolatrous nature of such worship often results in the Daemon Prince being heralded as a god that walks. Almost all Daemon Princes are incredibly proud, a side effect of having achieved their greatest ambition, and as such they often surround themselves with the most powerful warriors they can find; Chosen and a menagerie of warped monsters fill their hosts, forming a loathsome court over which the Daemon Prince reigns as an infernal monarch.

SOUL GRINDERS

When a daemon is banished, they may only return to the Mortal Realms after a given period of time, or until certain preconditions are met. For those whose desire for vengeance burns hottest, there is another way. These daemons make a pilgrimage to the Forge of Souls – the armoury of daemonkind, within the Realm of Chaos. Presenting themselves before the masters of the Forge, they speak the Oath of the Iron Pact, swearing themselves to their service in return for the chance to return to the physical plane. Those that do so are remade into a dreaded Soul Grinder. Their form swells with aetheric energy, while their lower bodies are replaced with clanking pistons and great mechanical legs. A Soul Grinder's arms end in hellish cannons or crushing machine-claws, and from their mouths they can project all manner of foul substances. A Soul Grinder scuttles across a battlefield with terrifying swiftness, its cannons raking the enemy while its augmented strength sees it crush even the Steam Tanks of the Ironweld Arsenal with ease.

'All the souls you will reap.
All of your spoils of war.
To be a keeper of the Forge.
But a trifle price for the boon that is
bestowed upon you.'

- A portion of the Iron Pact

Yet as with all things born of Chaos, there is a price for this dark rebirth. The masters of the Soul Forge forever desire more raw materials, and so the soul-price they demand of a Soul Grinder is constantly rising. Should one of these daemonic war engines be destroyed, they will be offered another reincarnation at

a steeper price. So do many Soul Grinders bind themselves eternally to the Soul Forge, forever chasing release from a servitude that they themselves created.

SLAUGHTERBRUTES

There is no room in a Slaughterbrute's mind for anything save thoughts of its next violent outburst. Each of its many limbs ends in razor-sharp claws that can slice through stone or armour with ease, and its monstrous jaws are wide enough to swallow an ogre whole. When raised to the heights of battle-fury a Slaughterbrute is an almost unstoppable force of destruction, its physical brawn and boundless rage spelling the doom for any unfortunate enough to catch the beast's attention.

Slaughterbrutes cannot be controlled through conventional means, but instead must be dominated with enchanted blades of binding. This is no easy feat, for the blade must be driven into a Slaughterbrute's spine to take effect, and such requires getting close to the beast in the first place. Those who succeed find that the creature inherits a measure of their new master's skill, rendering it even more lethal. There is, however, a downside: should the champion be slain, or stray too far away from their charge, then the beast will launch into an unstoppable rampage that ends only in death or through being bound once more. Those around a frenzied Slaughterbrute must hope that it chooses to vent its wrath upon the foe, before its bloodthirsty attention falls upon them.

MUTALITH VORTEX BEASTS

The origins of the first Mutalith Vortex Beasts are impossible to guess at, for whatever they once were, they are now little more than embodiments of Chaos in all its insanity. Since their emergence during the Age of Chaos, many Vortex Beasts can be found dwelling towards the Perimeter Inimical of each realm where the power of magic waxes stronger. Some sorcerers have even deduced how to create

Vortex Beasts through great spells of flesh-shaping, a process that is truly horrific for those caught up in it.

A Vortex Beast's hide constantly ripples with mutating energies, and from its gaping maw tentacles – formed of the creature's innards – lash out to batter any who get in its way. The true threat a Vortex Beast poses to its foes, however, lies in its connection to the Realm of Chaos. Swirling above a Mutalith's back is a yawning portal to the domain of the Ruinous Powers, through which the beast can harness the raw stuff of Chaos. The results are unpredictable, but always devastating: enemies may find their limbs twisting backwards, their bones warping into writhing serpents, or their bodies turning inside out. If the Mutalith is aware of these effects it gives no sign, but to the Slaves to Darkness the Vortex Beasts are proof that there is no natural law that Chaos cannot subvert to suit its needs.

CHAOS SPAWN

Chaos Spawn are all that remains of those champions who attempted to walk the Path to Glory, yet could not bear the strain of the gods' many 'gifts'. Their muscles flow and swell, bones cracking and reshaping as additional limbs or staring eyes break out across their lumpen forms. Last to go is the champion's mind, persisting just long enough to recognise the monstrosity they have become. The best that can be hoped for these horrific creatures is that they are herded into battle and given the opportunity to end their tortured existence in death.

Some tribes, particularly those associated with the gods of fate, treat Spawn with something approaching a measure of respect, for they see such a ghoulish transformation as the ultimate expression of their deities' will. The Spawn would likely disagree, if it retained the ability to consider such notions; on occasion, however, a measure of the champion's former sentience may briefly return, the horror of their predicament driving them to greater madness as they lash out with toxic claws and lashing tentacles.

ECHOES OF ETERNITY

Daemon Princes are immortal champions of the Dark Gods who have sold their souls in return for power and an eternity of war. Yet each was once a mortal who reached the apex of the Path to Glory – and each is defined by the fell deeds of their former lives…

'No.' Tyrezha hisses the word. It leaves her bloodied lips as a whispered prayer, not the curse she'd hoped to spit into the night air. Around her, the forest burns, once a grove of resplendent life, now a raging monument to her defeat.

She stares up at her killer, looking into eyes she knows, set into a face she doesn't.

She can't speak after that one whisper, not even to deny again what she's seeing. The revelation has ruined her, thieving away the last of her strength.

Her killer looks down on her with eyes that gleam with malignant gratitude. Thanking her for this death. Grateful that she lies here now, her blood soaking into the soil, her body spine-snapped and twisted by the blade running through her.

Tyrezha has seen that gaze in crumbled fever-dreams, in visions too fragmented to be called memories. Those eyes she once knew, now set within a face of gaunt, blood-dappled horror.

The forest still burns. The flames of Tyrezha's failure dance and writhe, reflected within the monster's stare.

The dying warrior reaches for her helmet. Shaking fingers drag it free. Blood runs from her mouth with the effort, drawn up from her sundered guts. She manages it, though; she bares her face, her pale skin amber in the firelight.

Surrounded by the inferno, killer and killed look upon one another and see the truth.

'Tyrezha,' the daemon breathes.
'Leisa,' the dying warrior whispers back.

Malukhara has seen kingdoms rise and fall over the eternity that her god has granted her. If one believes the golden, hairless caste of poet-things that slink in her shadow, she has bathed in the tears of her foes and swallowed the bones of their children

whole. They recite sagas where she tore down the walls of shining cities and supped blood from the skulls of kings.

Her name is a curse in a hundred cultures and a prayer in a hundred more. In the city-state of Dargolesh, she is worshipped as the Lady of Shattered Mirrors. The nomadic clans of the Ocean of Dust – those last echoing bloodlines of the grand Besharaan Confederacy – name her in their creation myths as the Ashen Goddess. To the war-tribes of the Uruchii Reaches, many of whom raise their banners in her hordes now, she is The-Cry-that-Carves-the-Night.

And how much of this is true?

She is above such concerns. Sifting the truth from the poetic lies is something she leaves to lesser beings.

Among her own kind, when they form words with their physical forms instead of radiating meaning through emotion and posture and expression, she is Malukhara. That is the name inscribed upon the scrolls carried by her war-priests and artist-worshippers.

Whole empires have lived and died beneath her gaze, raised high by misplaced valour only to be brought low by reaving fire and sacred blades. She watched those kingdoms tumble into the tides of history with the same curdled, sluggish joy she feels watching this grove burn.

An anaemic joy. A hollow delight. Because it's never enough, never enough.

Every victory is tinged with enough bitterness to sour the taste of anything sweet. Every conquest comes at a cost. Every triumph over the bones of a kingdom brings new curses with the gifted blessings. A city razed is a loss of the souls that should've sung her glories to the stars. A champion slaughtered is a hero never to take up arms and kill in her cause. An empress brought into Malukhara's court is a soul she will regret not

tasting when it was at its ripest.

For every glory… Regret. Never enough. Never enough.

And somewhere, deep in the back of what passes for a mind that has been inhuman for millennia, in the seething melange of her thoughts, she craves…

…next time, next time there will be true joy.

All of this? This is what Malukhara knows. This is what she's seen. This is what she feels, when she lets herself feel at all.

But Leisa has seen none of this, felt none of this, because Leisa is dead.

As dead as the empire that birthed her.

'This cannot be.'

Malukhara's voice is, like the daemon herself, a fusion of feline grace and canine savagery. Even as she says the words, she knows they're a lie. She speaks them for the theatre of it, because revelation requires reaction. It is the way of things.

Truly, she doesn't know whether to weep with joy or shriek in rage. She has cracked skies with her fury before. Her sorrow has been the genesis of rivers. Or… are those memories just shards of her saga-slaves' doggerel melting into her fractured mind?

She doesn't know. For now, she doesn't care.

What she sees before, it cannot be. And yet, it is.

Of all the souls that the Storm God might steal. Of all the numberless shades that Sigmar could gather and hammer back into half-life.

'Tyrezha.' She makes the name a purr, a snarl, a growl, a caress.

But the impaled daughter of the Storm God has no words for her. Tyrezha's breathing comes in ragged heaves, each gasp something stolen. Malukhara admires her, in a way. How the warrior refuses to die, as if it were truly a choice she could make; how Tyrezha defies death by clinging to the last moments of her ruined life.

And why?

Because the Storm God makes his sons and daughters so very strong.

Malukhara smiles at the thought. The expression is barely more than a curl of the lush scar tissue that remains of her lips, but it's enough to part the ivory graveyard of her teeth. Saliva, corrosive and stinking of seawater, strings down from the malformation of her maw.

Pockmarks of that drool sizzle on Tyrezha's breastplate. The metal hisses. Black smoke curls up from where the daemon's saliva pitter-patters onto the broken bronze of the warrior's armour.

Even now, Malukhara doesn't feel true, unbroken joy. Not even with her sword driven through her enemy's ruined form and deep into the earth beneath. Not even as the iron of her blade, forged in a realm of unreality, drinks the blood beating from her foe's sundered heart.

It isn't pure joy, but for the first time in aeons, it's close, so close. Her tears drip along with her saliva, a vile rainfall to baptise her fallen foe.

She speaks four words. Three are a command, growled softly amidst the burning trees, and the last is a name sweetly purred.

'Sing for me, Tyrezha.'

The dying daughter of the Storm God answers by gripping the blade with her bloodied gauntlets, leaving red smears on the monstrous metal as she tries one last time to draw it out of her guts.

'Sing,' the daemoness drawls, grinning now.

She twists the blade in Tyrezha's impaled form. Shattered sigmarite plate squeals as she writhes, but she refuses to cry out. And, of course, Malukhara admires her for that, too. But it won't change her fate.

The daemon's vast wings open with the wet crackle of cramped sinews, then ripple like great sails of stinking canvas. Their motions fan the inferno's heat down at the dying warrior, along with a musky reek, something both sweet and foul, with an edge of animal filth. Malukhara can smell her own scent. Her own perfume.

She leans on the blade one last

time, driving it through the belly of the dying warrior, deeper into the earth below.

'Sing for me, the way you used to.' The daemon is laughing, weeping; a daemonic blend of both which in truth resembles neither.

'With your last breath… Sing for me, sister.'

Tyrezha's fingers slip down the blade, scraping as they weaken, then falling away. She looks up now because she's too bloodless to look aside. Her sister's eyes shine with saltwater tears, and the monster's mouth forms drooling stalactites of ropey acid.

Leisa, she thinks – and in the same moment, indivisible: Malukhara.

The ground beneath the daemon's undulating form blackens with the creature's touch, the earth crumbling to ash, disgorging the shells of desiccated insects leeched of life. The trees still burn with witchfire, the heat brutal enough to scorch sigmarite, but already they're falling, collapsing beneath the weight of a far bleaker corruption. Malukhara's armies scarcely even need to ravage the land; their demon-queen's presence is enough to corrode reality.

Sing for me, sister.

Once, she'd done just that. In another age. In another life. The younger sister singing for the elder; a princess singing for a queen. Another joy in a kingdom where sunlight beamed upon white towers.

Then came the shadows. Then came the Queenswar. Then—

Stormclouds roll, grey with haste, black with fury. They darken the land and bathe it in rain, too late, too late to do anything but hiss on the dying trees and pool on Tyrezha's open eyes.

Leisa… Malukhara…

Then there is darkness.

And then there is Light.

Malukhara rips her blade free of the body. The corpse jerks with the movement, spilling rainwater down its cheeks, and the daemoness bares her teeth at the wretched symbolism. If any of her saga-thralls had witnessed it, surely they'd weave it into another preaching harmony of omens and portents.

She withdraws from the body,

felinely cleaning her weapon with long rakes of her tongue, tasting Tyrezha's blood on her blade, swallowing splinters of a life that ended an epoch ago.

Leisa. A city of spires. A chanting populace.

Tyrezha. A smiling child. A singing sister.

A war for a throne. A knife in the night. A deed that couldn't be undone.

Thunder calls out from above, warning the world below. The daemoness stops licking. She lowers the sword. She knows what's coming. After a battle, there's always carrion to be claimed.

The Storm God's rage echoes across the realm – a chorus of lightning and thunder; that elemental theme of the falsest god – and where Sigmar's dead sons and slain daughters lay moments before, now there is nothing but charred earth.

Just as the Lord of Joy once exalted her, now the Storm God has drawn her sister's soul into his heavenly foundry, back for another tawdry attempt at forging life. For how long had Tyrezha been one of Sigmar's sacred slaves? Had the sisters already met without knowing, in the years since the Storm God threw open the Gates of Azyr?

No.

She senses – she knows – the answer is No.

Tonight was the second time Tyrezha died in her sister's shadow. The first was in an age before they counted the Ages, when sister slew sister for the right to rule a kingdom now remembered by no living soul.

And the second…

Malukhara finds herself weeping once again. Close, so close, to the memory of rapture. She will treasure this reunion forever.

Now she prays to a god that isn't her own. She prays with every imagined beat of her spiteful heart, beseeching the distant God-King in his heavenly city to reforge Tyrezha again. And again. And again.

Even the memory of rapture, even the echo of ecstasy, is a pleasure to be pursued.

And no blood has ever tasted sweeter than her sister's.

DENIZENS OF THE EIGHTPOINTS

The damned lands of the Eightpoints ring constantly to the clamour of war. Under the shadow of the Varanspire warbands battle for dominance, seeking triumph over each other and deadly monsters alike. Yet more terrible is when these warriors unite to assail the civilised lands, for their hard-won skill makes them fearsome adversaries.

WARBANDS OF THE EIGHTPOINTS

Across the centuries, members of many different Chaos-worshipping cultures have made an unholy pilgrimage to the Eightpoints to fight for the chance to join Archaon's conquering hosts. These warbands are as varied as the realms they originate from; the Splintered Fang are jungle-dwelling masters of poison, while the Unmade of Shyish practise gruesome self-mutilation to render themselves into more perfect vessels of torment. As with most Slaves to Darkness, these cultures' interpretations of Chaos are similarly divergent. While the Cypher Lords worship it as a protean essence of trickery and madness, the Untamed Beasts pay homage to a brutal deity known as the Devourer of Existence. Most renowned are the Spire Tyrants, for these are the warriors who have fought within the fighting pits of the Varanspire, and consider themselves to be favoured by the Everchosen himself – a debatable assertion, though one that lends them great fury in battle.

Most of the time, these warbands battle one another for supremacy in the blasted wilds and bloody gladiatorial arenas of the Eightpoints. With increasing regularity, however, they can be found in the armies of the Slaves to Darkness. The Ravagers in particular see many of these warriors flock to their banners, eager to share in the spoils of victory won by these conquering and far-ranging Hordes. Whether the warbands of a particular culture fight en masse, or warriors from across the realms come together beneath a powerful Godsworn Overlord, they fight ferociously to prove themselves to the Everchosen's champions and earn a place in his armies.

OGROID MYRMIDONS

Little is known of the mysterious ogroids. Long ago they were part of the hordes of Destruction, but became embroiled in a war against Gorkamorka. This is not particularly surprising, for the Twin-Headed God has forever relished violence, but the ogroids were too proud to accept defeat even at a deity's hand. In desperation, they turned to Chaos for the strength to triumph. To beg for aid further offended Gorkamorka's warrior principles. Soon orruks, ogors and even grots in their thousands strove to annihilate the ogroids. Only through fleeing into the most Chaos-tainted lands did they survive.

Despite their fearsome appearance, ogroids are no mere brutes. Some of their number became mystic Thaumaturges, but many instead follow the path of the Myrmidon. They devote themselves to the art of combat, wielding spiked shields and heavy spears with breathtaking skill. Any who accept a Myrmidon's challenge will receive a brief salute before being impaled by the deadly polearm. Should an ogroid be wounded, the runes carved across their body will glow with a hellish light, empowering the creature further. Ogroid Myrmidons often serve as masters of the fighting pits of the Eightpoints. Those who excel under the gaze of a Myrmidon often go on to achieve great glory, and so the warbands of the Eightpoints congregate around them, seeking to impress these battle-masters through their own feats of arms.

MINDSTEALER SPHIRANXES

A Mindstealer Sphiranx delights in plundering secrets from the mind of its prey. The source of this invasive telepathic power is the third eye upon the leonine creature's forehead. This is no natural quirk, but an unholy boon gained at terrible cost. Once, the Sphiranxes were an order of Hyshian mystics. Though they possessed no natural magical talent, they held considerable affinity for the guardianship of arcane artefacts, and served Teclis as custodians of esoteric treasures. Yet little by little, the Sphiranxes' noble ideals were polluted. They grew to crave sorcerous power, their jealousy fed by insidious whispers from the Changer of the Ways. In frustration, the High Bibliarch of the Sphiranxes struck a dark bargain. The third eye bestowed upon the creatures allowed them to peer into the minds of others and pluck knowledge from within, but severed all other connections to the aether.

Compelled to drain the knowledge from all they encountered, the rush of information eventually drove the Sphiranxes mad. Hounded by Teclis and the military orders of Hysh, they slunk away into the dark corners of the Eightpoints to seethe over the perceived injustices done to them. Only by the will of a great warlord do the Sphiranxes emerge from their lairs. They are swift despite their size, capable of pouncing upon and crushing foes before leaping away. Yet it is the sinister psychic power of the Sphiranxes that makes them so dangerous. Coldly intelligent, they revel in casting themselves into their enemies' minds; a warrior may suddenly forget years of training, or be immobilised as old traumas are relived. This helplessness amuses a Sphiranx greatly in the moments before their victims are torn asunder.

FOMOROID CRUSHERS

Fomoroid Crushers have long possessed an affinity for stonecraft. They can pull apart a structure with remarkable ease, swinging chunks of masonry to crush the life from their enemies Once, they served as a builder caste for one of the great civilisations of the Allpoints. Though skilled masons, the fomoroids won little respect from their masters. Treated as veritable slaves, eventually they could bear it no more, and launched a rebellion against their overseers. After a brutal conflict that saw majestic works of architecture destroyed, the fomoroids achieved victory over their old masters. Freedom lay within their grasp.

Then came the Nexus Wars. Like all other inhabitants of the Allpoints, the fomoroids were no match for the armies of the Everchosen. Knowing that no physical prison could hold the creatures, Archaon worked a grand sorcery that bound them in mind rather than body. With a cruel laugh the Everchosen absorbed them into his vast armies, or otherwise cast them into the cells of his fighting pits, amused that those who had built could now only destroy. A fomoroid's monstrous strength renders it a terrifying foe, yet not everything of their past has been lost. When the day is done, the creatures drag the carcasses of their victims back into the dark depths of their cells. There, works of primitive art cover the walls as the creatures' sentience struggles for dominance. Where once they raised glorious empires, now they can build only with the materials of death, mosaics of teeth and paintings wrought from splattered gore a constant reminder of all they have lost.

The march of ruin is unstoppable. In pursuit of glory the Slaves to Darkness crush all who stand before them, each slain foe an offering to the Chaos Gods.

DIABOLIC GLORY

From ironclad legions of Chaos Warriors to hideously mutated warbeasts, few Citadel Miniatures ranges are as varied as the Slaves to Darkness. Here we present a showcase of fell warriors, foul beasts and dark-hearted champions expertly painted by Games Workshop's very own 'Eavy Metal Team and Design Studio army painters.

Under the gaze of their iron-willed Overlord and the champions of the Chaos Gods, the Slaves to Darkness bring war to the civilised lands of the Mortal Realms.

Chaos Lord on Karkadrak

Chaos Knight

Doom Knight

Where the Varanguard ride, the will of Archaon rides with them, inspiring the dark tribes to new heights of bloodshed.

Aspiring Champion with Mark of Khorne

Chaos Warrior with Mark of Tzeentch

Chaos Warrior with Mark of Nurgle

Chaos Warrior with Mark of Slaanesh

Chaos Warriors

Archaon the Everchosen, Exalted Grand Marshal of the Apocalypse

Warbands of Darkoath and the Untamed Beasts raid a crumbling temple of its long-hidden treasures.

The Varanguard are Archaon's favoured champions, each a fearsome lord of Chaos in their own right.

The Gaunt Summoners are bound to the will of Archaon, riding to battle atop bizarre Discs of Tzeentch.

Cabalist armies are led by sorcerer covens, and use the blood of barbarous tribesmen to fuel their dark rituals.

Corvus Cabal

Cypher Lords

The Unmade

Iron Golem

Spire Tyrants

Untamed Beasts

Splintered Fang

The Corvus Cabal strike from unexpected angles, descending to tear their foes asunder and pick clean the corpses.

Thronged with monsters and the beasts of the wastes, Be'lakor's Despoiler Horde brings terror to the Mortal Realms.

Daemon Prince

Fomoroid Crusher

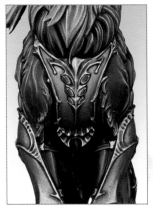

Mindstealer Sphiranx

59

In the presence of a Warshrine, the Slaves to Darkness are empowered by the manifest favour of the Chaos Gods.

WARRIORS OF THE GODS

Driven by an insatiable lust to conquer, and in so doing attract the favour of the Chaos Gods, the Slaves to Darkness are one of the most feared forces in all the Mortal Realms. The following pages give an example of a collection of these ferocious warriors, and how you might go about choosing units to include in your own.

With any Age of Sigmar army, it's a good idea to have a vision of what sort of force you want to build before amassing your collection. In the case of the Slaves to Darkness, this is doubly important. The Hordes of these ruinous warriors are all very different, and making the best use of their abilities will be key to your battle strategy. On the following pages we present just one way of preparing your collection for battle.

After considering the various options available to us – and consulting the Dark Gods for their wisdom, of course – we've decided to make this collection into a Ravagers army (pg 70). As the most commonly found Hordes in the Mortal Realms this make a lot of narrative sense, as well as giving us powerful tactical options on the tabletop.

With this decided, our next task is to select a mighty general to walk the Path to Glory and lead our warriors to victory. A Chaos Lord on Karkadrak fits the bill nicely, and will provide a solid core to our force that is capable of smashing aside the enemy with bone-breaking charges.

Ravager armies are built around powerful heroes, and so we've included several such champions to bolster our forces. A Darkoath Warqueen and Chieftain will help power up our infantry, as well as being potent fighters in their own right. A Chaos Sorcerer Lord provides magical support, while an Ogroid Myrmidon will lead our Cultists to glory (or, at least, a worthy death).

Next we need a solid core of infantry. Two units of Chaos Warriors forms an excellent core to our battleline,

while units of Untamed Beasts and Spire Tyrants can hunt down the foe and pick off stragglers. With these we have a good mixture of killing power and objective-taking ability, especially when they are joined by the heroes we've chosen. To swing the odds further in our favour, a Chaos Warshrine can channel the power of the gods and bless our warriors, enhancing their already formidable skills further.

Though deadly, Chaos infantry are typically not the fastest units around, so we've included several warbands of swift cavalry and chariots to address this shortfall. Two units of Chaos Knights will help drive home the impact of our charge, especially when backed up by the brutal bludgeoning power of a Gorebeast Chariot. Some

Marauder Horsemen, meanwhile, can dash onto far-flung objectives and ride down vulnerable enemies – especially when backed up by a fleet Chaos Chariot. Put together, these units help balance out our force and will be particularly useful for tying up enemy ranged units, allowing our infantry to cross the board and get stuck into glorious melee.

The collection we've assembled gives us various options in terms of warscroll battalions. By grouping our Chaos Warriors, Knights, Marauder Horsemen and chariots under our Chaos Lord, we can form the fearsome Godsworn Champions of Ruin – or maybe add in the Warshrine as well to create a Godswrath Warband. Alternatively, we could bring our cavalry, chariots and Chaos Lord together as a

Ruinbringer Warband to maximise the power of our heavy mounted contingent. As we play more games we can choose whichever of these battalions we like best, ensuring that we have a competitive army that will also be great fun to paint.

1. Chaos Lord on Karkadrak
2. Darkoath Warqueen
3. Darkoath Chieftain
4. Chaos Sorcerer Lord
5. Ogroid Myrmidon
6. Chaos Warriors
7. Chaos Warriors
8. Untamed Beasts
9. Spire Tyrants
10. Chaos Knights
11. Chaos Knights
12. Marauder Horsemen
13. Chaos Chariot
14. Gorebeast Chariot
15. Chaos Warshrine

61

PAINTING YOUR SLAVES TO DARKNESS

With a wide variety of models and textures, and a wealth of colour schemes to experiment with, the Slaves to Darkness are an incredibly rewarding force to paint whatever your level of skill. The following pages contain helpful hints and tips to get your Slaves to Darkness collection ready to conquer the Mortal Realms.

The sheer variety of models in the Slaves to Darkness range makes them a collector's dream. Whether you want to field a small force of elite champions, a vast horde of raging barbarians, a bizarre menagerie of monsters or anything in between, you'll find something for you in the followers of the Dark Gods.

Yet although the Slaves to Darkness strike terror into their enemies on the battlefield, painting them needn't be quite so intimidating. The Citadel Paint System contains all the colours a burgeoning champion of the gods could hope for, and with the aid of a few simple tricks and techniques your legions will be ready for battle in no time.

You should always feel free to paint your models however you wish. Each Chaos God has their traditional colours, but you shouldn't feel bound by these. Remember that the Slaves to Darkness represent the greatest portion of humanity in the Mortal Realms, and each tribe venerates Chaos in their own way. If you want to paint your Khorne-marked Warriors with deep brass armour and red filigree, you absolutely can. If you wish to collect a Marauder tribe from Aqshy marked with bright flame tattoos, then go for it!

So long as you are happy with the result, and everything is clear to your opponent on the tabletop, then the sky is the limit. The following pages contain some helpful hints to get you started. Beyond that, let your Chaos-touched imagination run wild!

WARHAMMER TV

Warhammer TV's painting tutorials have insights for everyone, as they show you how to paint Citadel Miniatures from start to finish. The guides are available for free on games-workshop.com, and can also be watched via the Warhammer TV YouTube channel. Why not take a moment to check them out?

BLACK ARMOUR

Using Chaos Black Spray as an undercoat makes this initial stage quick and easy. Paint any areas that were missed by the spray with Abaddon Black.

When the undercoat is dry, carefully paint the edges and raised detail of the armour plates with fine lines of Dark Reaper. An S Layer Brush is ideal for this step.

Finish by painting even finer lines of Administratum Grey on top of the previous highlights, making sure to leave some of the Dark Reaper showing underneath.

GOLD DETAILS

Paint the sections of gold armour using an S Base Brush and Retributor Armour.

Now, give them an all-over shade of Agrax Earthshade, applied with an M Shade Brush.

Next, paint the raised sections of the armour plate with Auric Armour Gold.

Finish by applying Runefang Steel to the most prominent edges using an S Artificer Layer Brush.

RED CLOTH

1

2

3

4

Begin by applying a basecoat of Khorne Red with an S Base Brush. Use two or three thin coats for a smooth finish.

Next apply a Shade of Druchii Violet, focusing on the folds and holes in the cloth while avoiding the raised areas.

Using an S Layer Brush, apply lines of Evil Sunz Scarlet to the edges of the cloth and the sharpest raised folds.

Finish up with even finer lines of Fire Dragon Bright to really define the sharp edges of the cloth.

DETAILS

Leadbelcher (basecoat), Agrax Earthshade (shade), 1:2 mix of Gore-grunta Fur and Contrast Medium in the occasional recess.

Celestra Grey (basecoat), 1:1 mix of Nuln Oil and Lahmian Medium (shade), Celestra Grey (layer), Grey Seer (highlight).

Ushabti Bone (basecoat), 1:1 mix of Reikland Fleshshade and Lahmian Medium (shade), Ushabti Bone (layer).

Leadbelcher (basecoat), Nuln Oil (shade), Runefang Steel (edge highlight).

SKIN VARIANTS

Over a basecoat of Grey Seer, apply a carefully controlled coat of Space Wolves Grey Contrast paint.

This skin tone was painted simply by applying a controlled coat of Guilliman Flesh over a Grey Seer basecoat.

Grey Seer (basecoat), 1:1 mix of Darkoath Flesh and Contrast Medium, Pallid Wych Flesh (highlight).

Bloodreaver Flesh (basecoat), Nuln Oil (shade), Knight-Questor Flesh then Cadian Fleshtone (edge highlights).

MUTATED STEED FLESH

1

2

3

4

First, apply a basecoat of Mechanicus Standard Grey using an S Base Brush.

When this is dry, take an M Shade Brush and shade the grey areas all over with Nuln Oil.

Use an S Layer Brush to apply Stormvermin Fur to the wrinkles and raised details.

Using the same brush, paint finer highlights of Karak Stone to define the steed's sharpest features.

MARK OF KHORNE - RED ARMOUR

1

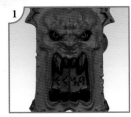

Start by basecoating the armour plating with Khorne Red.

2

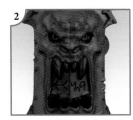

Next, carefully apply Nuln Oil to the recesses to create some contrast.

3

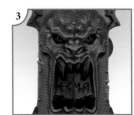

Use Evil Sunz Scarlet to highlight the raised edges and raised details.

4

Lastly, apply a finer highlight of Fire Dragon Bright to these same areas.

MARK OF KHORNE - DETAILS

Abaddon Black (basecoat), Incubi Darkness (edge highlight), Thunderhawk Blue then Administratum Grey (edge highlights)

Corvus Black (basecoat), Eshin Grey (edge highlight), Dawnstone (edge highlight)

Bronze: Fulgurite Copper (basecoat), Agrax Earthshade (shade), Skullcrusher Brass (layer), Stormhost Silver (edge highlight)

Horns: Rakarth Flesh (basecoat), 1:1 mix of Agrax Earthshade and Lahmian Medium (shade), Rakarth Flesh (lines on horns)

MARK OF TZEENTCH - BLUE-GREEN ARMOUR

1

Basecoat the armour with a coat of Leadbelcher.

2

Apply a few coats of Aethermatic Blue, allowing each coat to dry before applying the next.

3

Carefully apply Warp Lightning around the rivets and into the recesses between the armour plates.

4

Finish up by applying an edge highlight of Stormhost Silver.

MARK OF TZEENTCH - DETAILS

Incubi Darkness (basecoat), Nuln Oil (shade), Kabalite Green then Sybarite Green (edge highlights)

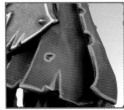

Screamer Pink (basecoat), Nuln Oil (recess shade), Pink Horror then Cadian Fleshtone (edge highlights)

Leadbelcher (basecoat), Druchii Violet (shade), Stormhost Silver (edge highlight)

Rakarth Flesh (basecoat), 1:1 mix of Drakenhof Nightshade and Lahmian Medium (shade)

MARK OF NURGLE – GREEN ARMOUR

1

Start with an undercoat of Death Guard Green Spray or Base paint.

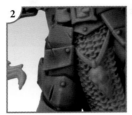

2

Next, apply a 1:1 mix of Militarum Green and Contrast Medium all over the armour.

3

Use Straken Green to apply edge highlights to the raised areas.

4

Finally, use Nurgling Green to apply further edge highlights.

MARK OF NURGLE – DETAILS

Leadbelcher (basecoat), Agrax Earthshade (shade), Ryza Rust (stipple), Stormhost Silver (edge highlight)

Incubi Darkness (basecoat), Nuln Oil, (recess shade), Mechanicus Standard Grey then Administratum Grey (edge highlights)

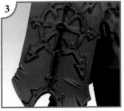

Brass Scorpion (basecoat), Agrax Earthshade (shade), Stormhost Silver (edge highlight)

1:1 Sotek Green and Lahmian Medium mix, in patches, to simulate verdigris.

MARK OF SLAANESH – PURPLE ARMOUR

1

Apply Naggaroth Night as a basecoat.

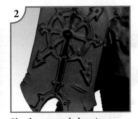

2

Shade around the rivets and inside the cuts and dents with Black Templar.

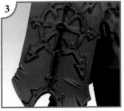

3

Highlight the edges and raised detail using Phoenician Purple.

4

Apply a finer highlight to these same areas with Kakophoni Purple.

MARK OF SLAANESH – DETAILS

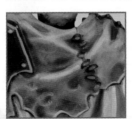

Cadian Fleshtone (basecoat), 1:1 mix of Carroburg Crimson and Lahmian Medium (recess shade), Cadian Fleshtone (highlight)

Celestra Grey (basecoat), 1:1 mix of Dawnstone and Lahmian Medium (recess shade), Ulthuan Grey (edge highlight)

Kislev Flesh (basecoat), 1:1 mix of Druchii Violet and Lahmian Medium (shade), Kislev Flesh (layer), Screaming Skull (highlight)

Retributor Armour (basecoat), Reikland Fleshshade Gloss (shade), Auric Armour Gold (layer), Stormhost Silver (edge highlight)

ARMIES OF DARKNESS

This battletome contains all of the rules you need to field your Slaves to Darkness miniatures on the battlefields of the Mortal Realms, from a host of exciting allegiance abilities to a range of warscrolls and warscroll battalions. The rules are split into the following sections.

ALLEGIANCE ABILITIES

This section describes the allegiance abilities available to a Slaves to Darkness army. The rules for using allegiance abilities can be found in the *Warhammer Age of Sigmar Core Book*.

SLAVES TO DARKNESS

Battle traits available to all Slaves to Darkness armies, and spells available to **Wizards** in Slaves to Darkness armies (pg 68-69).

DAMNED LEGIONS

Additional battle traits, command traits and artefacts of power available to Slaves to Darkness armies that have been given the appropriate keyword (see the Damned Legions battle trait, opposite).

BATTLEPLANS

This section includes a new narrative battleplan that can be played with a Slaves to Darkness army (pg 78).

PATH TO GLORY

This section contains rules for using your Slaves to Darkness collection in Path to Glory campaigns (pg 80-83).

WARSCROLLS

This section includes all of the warscrolls you will need to play games of Warhammer Age of Sigmar with your Slaves to Darkness miniatures. There are three types of warscroll included in this section:

WARSCROLL BATTALIONS

These are formations made up of several Slaves to Darkness units that combine their strengths to gain powerful new abilities (pg 84-87).

WARSCROLLS

A warscroll for each unit is included here. The rules for using a Slaves to Darkness unit, along with its characteristics and abilities, are detailed on its warscroll (pg 88-116).

ENDLESS SPELL WARSCROLLS

There are three endless spell warscrolls that detail the rules for unique and powerful spells that can be summoned by Slaves to Darkness **Wizards** (pg 117-118). The rules for playing games with endless spells can be found in the *Warhammer Age of Sigmar Core Book* and in *Warhammer Age of Sigmar: Malign Sorcery*.

PITCHED BATTLE PROFILES

This section contains Pitched Battle profiles for the units, warscroll battalions and endless spells in this book (pg 119-120).

ALLIES

This section has a list of the allies a Slaves to Darkness army can include (pg 120).

ALLEGIANCE ABILITIES
SLAVES TO DARKNESS

BATTLE TRAITS – BANE OF THE MORTAL REALMS

DAMNED LEGIONS

The hordes of Chaos wage war in all manner of ways, driven by the dark desires of their Overlords.

After you have chosen the Slaves to Darkness allegiance for your army, you must choose a Damned Legion keyword from the list below. All **Slaves to Darkness** units in your army gain that keyword, and you can use that Damned Legion's allegiance abilities in addition to the Slaves to Darkness allegiance abilities.

- **Ravagers** (pg 70-71)
- **Cabalists** (pg 72-73)
- **Despoilers** (pg 74-75)
- **Host of the Everchosen** (pg 76-77)

If a unit already has a Damned Legion keyword on its warscroll different to the one you chose, it cannot gain another. You can still include that unit in your army, but you cannot use the allegiance abilities for its Damned Legion.

AURA OF CHAOS

An aura of dark power surrounds the champions of Chaos, bolstering those who share their devotion.

Each **Slaves to Darkness Hero** in a Slaves to Darkness army has one of the following Aura of Chaos abilities. The Aura of Chaos a **Hero** has is determined by its Mark of Chaos keyword: **Khorne Heroes** have the Aura of Khorne, **Tzeentch Heroes** have the Aura of Tzeentch, **Nurgle Heroes** have the Aura of Nurgle, **Slaanesh Heroes** have the Aura of Slaanesh, and **Undivided Heroes** have the Aura of Chaos Undivided.

If you select a unit with more than one Mark of Chaos keyword to be part of your army, you must pick which one will apply to that unit for the duration of the battle.

Aura of Khorne: *The spirit of war can only be honoured on the battlefield, and those who bear the blood-mark fight with a savage fury.*

You can re-roll hit rolls of 1 for attacks made with melee weapons by friendly **Slaves to Darkness Khorne** units wholly within 12" of this model. In addition, if this model is a general, add 1 to wound rolls for attacks made with melee weapons by friendly **Slaves to Darkness Khorne** units wholly within 12" of this model.

Aura of Tzeentch: *Followers of the fated paths are able to foretell and defend against enemy attacks, and often prove resilient against wild magic.*

You can re-roll save rolls of 1 for attacks that target friendly **Slaves to Darkness Tzeentch** units wholly within 12" of this model. In addition, if this model is a general, each time a friendly **Slaves to Darkness Tzeentch** unit wholly within 12" of this model is affected by a spell or endless spell, you can roll a dice. If you do so, on a 5+, ignore the effects of that spell or endless spell on that unit.

Aura of Nurgle: *Warriors who worship the cycle of life and death find their weapons coated in virulent toxins, their coming obscured behind clouds of buzzing flies.*

If the unmodified wound roll for an attack made with a melee weapon by a friendly **Slaves to Darkness Nurgle** unit wholly within 12" of any friendly models with this ability is 6, add 1 to the damage inflicted by that attack. In addition, if this model is a general, subtract 1 from hit rolls for attacks made with missile weapons that target friendly **Slaves to Darkness Nurgle** units wholly within 12" of this model.

Aura of Slaanesh: *The devotees of ecstasy are filled with manic energy, and can harness it to move and fight with shocking swiftness.*

If the unmodified hit roll for an attack made with a melee weapon by a friendly **Slaves to Darkness Slaanesh** unit wholly within 12" of this model is 6, that attack scores 2 hits on the target instead of 1. Make a wound and save roll for each hit. In addition, if this model is a general, you can re-roll run and charge rolls for friendly **Slaves to Darkness Slaanesh** units wholly within 12" of this model.

Aura of Chaos Undivided: *Those warriors who have yet to pledge their souls to a single deity are amongst the most zealous walkers of the Path to Glory, and are fearless in their pursuit of greatness.*

Do not take battleshock tests for friendly **Slaves to Darkness Undivided** units wholly within 12" of this model. In addition, if this model is a general, roll a dice each time you allocate a wound or mortal wound to a friendly **Slaves to Darkness Undivided** unit wholly within 12" of this model. On a 6, that wound or mortal wound is negated.

EYE OF THE GODS

The Slaves to Darkness seek to attract the notice of the gods through performing great deeds in battle. To court the gaze of these beings is perilous, yet those who prove worthy are made mighty indeed.

At the end of the combat phase, if any attacks made by a friendly **Slaves to Darkness Hero** that has the **Eye of the Gods** keyword destroyed any enemy **Heroes** or **Monsters** in that phase, you can make 1 roll on the Eye of the Gods table below for that friendly **Hero**.

Rewards gained by rolling on this table apply for the rest of the battle. Duplicate rewards are treated as 'Snubbed by the Gods' instead.

2D6   Reward

2   Spawndom: *Unable to bear the strain of so many 'gifts', the champion's body is twisted into a new and hideous form.*

You can add 1 **Slaves to Darkness Chaos Spawn** to your army. If you do so, set up 1 **Slaves to Darkness Chaos Spawn** model within 1" of this **Hero**, then this **Hero** is slain. If you do not add a **Slaves to Darkness Chaos Spawn** to your army, this **Hero** suffers D3 mortal wounds.

3   Slaughterer's Strength: *The champion's body swells with daemonic energies, their blows sundering even the most formidable armour.*

Pick 1 of this **Hero**'s melee weapons. Improve the Rend characteristic of that weapon by 1.

4   Murderous Mutation: *Whether a sharp horn or lashing tentacle, this mutation proves most useful in the press of a melee.*

Pick 1 of this **Hero**'s melee weapons. Add 1 to the Attacks characteristic of that weapon.

5   Iron Flesh: *The champion's skin warps into living metal, blunting all but the mightiest blows.*

Add 1 to save rolls for attacks that target this **Hero**.

6   Flames of Chaos: *The champion is surrounded by a corona of multihued flame that devours hostile arcane energies.*

Each time this **Hero** is affected by a spell or endless spell you can roll a dice. If you do so, on a 4+, ignore the effects of that spell or endless spell on this **Hero**.

7   Snubbed by the Gods: *The gods demand more from the champion before granting their boon.*

This reward has no effect.

8   Unholy Resilience: *Fortified by the dark power of Chaos, the champion becomes almost immune to pain.*

Roll a dice each time you allocate a wound or mortal wound to this **Hero**. On a 5+, that wound or mortal wound is negated.

9-10   Daemonic Legions: *The champion's deeds draw the daemons of their god to the battlefield.*

You can add 1 of the following units to your army. The unit you add is determined by this **Hero**'s Mark of Chaos. Set up the unit wholly within 12" of this **Hero** and more than 9" from any enemy units.

- **Khorne:** 10 Bloodletters
- **Nurgle:** 10 Plaguebearers
- **Slaanesh:** 10 Daemonettes
- **Tzeentch:** 10 Pink Horrors
- **Undivided:** 6 Furies

11-12   Dark Apotheosis: *The champion has repeatedly excelled themselves in the eyes of their patron god, and upon them is bestowed the dark glory of daemonhood.*

You can add a **Slaves to Darkness Daemon Prince** to your army. If you do so, set it up within 1" of this **Hero** then remove this **Hero** from play (they do not count as slain).

If the **Hero** had the **Undivided** keyword, the **Daemon Prince** must instead have one of the following Mark of Chaos keywords: **Khorne, Nurgle, Slaanesh** or **Tzeentch.** Otherwise, the **Daemon Prince** must have the same Mark of Chaos keyword that the **Hero** had.

The **Daemon Prince** keeps any command traits and artefacts of power that the **Hero** had. If the **Hero** was a **Wizard**, the **Daemon Prince** is a **Wizard**, can make the same number of casting, dispelling and unbinding attempts, and knows the same spells. If the **Hero** was your general, the **Daemon Prince** is now your general.

If you do not set up a **Slaves to Darkness Daemon Prince**, you can heal up to D3 wounds allocated to this **Hero**.

SPELL LORE – LORE OF THE DAMNED

You can choose or roll for one spell from the following table for each **Slaves to Darkness Wizard** in a Slaves to Darkness army.

D6 Spell

1 Binding Damnation: *At the caster's urging, tendrils of raw Chaos burst from the tortured ground, entwining the limbs of their enemies and rendering them easy prey.*

Binding Damnation has a casting value of 7. If successfully cast, pick 1 enemy unit within 12" of the caster and visible to them. Until your next hero phase, that unit fights at the end of the combat phase.

2 Spite-tongue Curse: *Uttering the foul syllables of the Dark Tongue until blood pours from their mouth, the caster beseeches the Chaos Gods to destroy their enemies – though such pacts carry with them a terrible cost…*

Spite-tongue Curse has a casting value of 3. If successfully cast, pick 1 enemy unit within 12" of the caster and visible to them. That unit suffers 3 mortal wounds. If the casting roll is unsuccessful or the spell is unbound, the caster suffers 3 mortal wounds.

3 Whispers of Chaos: *The caster projects treasonous whispers into the minds of the foe, compelling even the closest comrades to turn upon one another in a furious rage.*

Whispers of Chaos has a casting value of 7. If successfully cast, pick 1 enemy unit within 12" of the caster and visible to them. Roll a number of dice equal to the number of models in that unit. For each 6, that unit suffers 1 mortal wound. If any models from that unit are slain by this spell, that unit cannot move until the start of your next hero phase.

4 Mask of Darkness: *A shroud of black mist snatches up the caster's allies, only to have them reappear to strike from a new and unexpected angle.*

Mask of Darkness has a casting value of 7. If successfully cast, pick 1 friendly **Mortal Slaves to Darkness** unit wholly within 12" of the caster and visible to them. Remove that unit from the battlefield and then set it up again anywhere on the battlefield more than 9" from any enemy units. That unit cannot move in the following movement phase.

5 Call to Glory: *The caster infuses one of their allies with a measure of infernal power, granting them the strength to take on the mightiest foes.*

Call to Glory has a casting value of 5. If successfully cast, pick 1 friendly **Slaves to Darkness Hero** wholly within 12" of the caster and visible to them. You can re-roll hit and wound rolls for attacks made by that **Hero** if target is a **Hero** or **Monster** until your next hero phase.

6 Ruinous Vigour: *Choosing a worthy beast from amongst the horde, the caster imbues the creature with monstrous strength, allowing it to fight on in spite of its wounds for a time.*

Ruinous Vigour has a casting value of 6. If successfully cast, pick 1 friendly **Slaves to Darkness Monster** wholly within 12" of the caster and visible to them. Until your next hero phase, when you look up a value on that **Monster**'s damage table, it is treated as if it has suffered 0 wounds.

RAVAGERS

Under the command of powerful warlords, the Ravagers spread carnage across the Mortal Realms. Their armies are vast, bolstered by countless warbands and tribes competing to claim the lion's share of the glory, and the constant competition for dominance amongst their leaders has forged truly formidable champions.

True to their name, the Ravagers have long been a plague upon civilisation. The majority of Chaos-held territory within the Mortal Realms can be attributed to the conquests of the Ravager Hordes, and when the armies of the Dark Gods gather in force it is they who make up the bulk of those forces. Whether they all worship the same deity or pay homage to a range of patrons, Ravager Hordes are inevitably numerous. Their numbers are predominantly provided by the large barbarian tribes who swear themselves to champions who have proven themselves worthy, as well as elite cores of bodyguards and armoured legions that surround the Horde's Godsworn Overlord. The champions of the Ravagers are, by necessity, charismatic and dangerous individuals

– they must be, for it is entirely expected amongst the Ravagers that a warrior will launch a leadership challenge against their warlord without warning should they believe them to be unworthy. Their traits and skills have been honed over a lifetime of brutal warfare, and at their beck and call are barbarous warbands willing to fight and die for the glory of the Ruinous Powers. The Darkoath in particular have found kindred spirits in the marauding armies of the Ravagers, and many such Hordes now fight to fulfil the great pacts sworn by these savage warleaders. Regardless of their motives or methods, the Ravagers are devoted servants of the gods, and they will never cease their warmongering while a single enemy of Chaos remains.

BATTLE TRAITS – ARMIES OF THE DARK TRIBES

GLORY FOR THE TAKING

The lords and chieftains of a Ravager Horde relentlessly tread the Path to Glory, seeking to prove themselves the mightiest warrior and thus the most worthy to lead.

If your general is not a **DAEMON PRINCE**, you can pick 1 command trait for up to 5 different friendly **RAVAGERS HEROES** (excluding **DAEMON PRINCES**) in addition to the command trait your general can have. You must pick a different command trait for each of these **HEROES**, and none of them can have more than 1 command trait. You can use these command traits for these **HEROES** even though they are not your general.

At the start of your hero phase, you can pick 1 friendly **RAVAGERS HERO** (excluding **DAEMON PRINCES**) that is on the battlefield and has a command trait to stake their claim as warlord. If you do so, that **HERO** becomes the army general until your next hero phase.

COMMAND ABILITY

A **RAVAGERS** general has the following command ability:

Rally the Tribes: *Seizing the moment to prove their supremacy, one of the horde's commanders lets loose a terrifying battle cry, calling more of their blade-sworn warriors to their side.*

You can use this command ability at the end of your movement phase. If you do so, pick the model that is currently your general. The same model cannot be picked more than once per battle. That model rallies 1 unit of 10 **CHAOS MARAUDERS**, 1 unit of 5 **CHAOS MARAUDER HORSEMEN** or 1 **CULTISTS** unit of up to 10 models to the battlefield. The unit is added to your army, and must be set up wholly within 6" of the edge of the battlefield and more than 9" from any enemy units.

COMMAND TRAITS – RUINOUS OVERLORDS
Ravagers Hero general only.

D6	Command Trait

1 Bolstered by Hate: *This general is imbued with an unnatural loathing that manifests as a vile nimbus of Chaos energy.*

Add 2 to this general's Wounds characteristic.

2 Unquestioned Resolve: *Bands of unruly warriors jump at this general's commands.*

Once per turn, you can use the At the Double, Forward to Victory or Inspiring Presence command ability without a command point being spent if the friendly unit is a **Cultists** unit within 12" of this general.

3 Favoured of the Pantheon: *The gods watch this warlord's deeds particularly closely.*

You can add or subtract 2 from the result of any rolls made for this general on the Eye of the Gods table (pg 68).

4 Eternal Vendetta: *Burning in the chest of this general is an undying hatred for the followers of Sigmar's godly allies.*

You can re-roll wound rolls for attacks made by this general. In addition, you can re-roll hit rolls for attacks made by this general that target **Order** units.

5 Flames of Spite: *Chaotic fire clings to the form of this warlord, leaping out to immolate foes.*

If the unmodified wound roll for an attack made by this general is 6, the target suffers 1 mortal wound in addition to any normal damage.

6 Master of Deception: *This champion uses guile and trickery to wrong-foot their enemies.*

Subtract 1 from hit rolls for attacks made with melee weapons that target this general.

ARTEFACTS OF POWER – TROPHIES OF CONQUEST
Ravagers Hero only.

D6	Artefact

1 Hellfire Sword: *This blade was made from a single searing flame that was hammered into material form and quenched in the blood of a fire-djinn.*

Once per battle, in your shooting phase, you can pick 1 enemy unit within 8" of the bearer and visible to them. That unit suffers D3 mortal wounds.

2 Blasphemous Cuirass: *The profane inscriptions and grim fetishes adorning this breastplate project an unholy aura that provides the most devout Chaos worshippers with hellish resilience.*

Roll a dice each time a mortal wound is allocated to the bearer. On a 5+, that mortal wound is negated.

3 Helm of the Oppressor: *The blackened bone plates of this helmet induce soul-piercing dread in the champion's enemies.*

Subtract 1 from the Bravery characteristic of enemy units while they are within 6" of the bearer.

4 Cloak of the Relentless Conqueror: *The daemon-mites bound within each fibre of this time-worn cloak drive the bearer endlessly on, until victory is achieved or death claims them.*

You can re-roll charge rolls for the bearer.

5 Mark of the High-favoured: *This warrior's chosen deity pays close attention to his actions on the battlefield, their unholy power radiating in waves around the champion.*

Friendly **Ravagers** units are affected by the bearer's Aura of Chaos ability while they are wholly within 18" of the bearer.

6 Desecrator Gauntlets: *The snaking trails of balefire that flicker around these paired iron gloves corrupt and destroy that which is sacred or imbued with magic.*

Subtract 2 from casting rolls for enemy **Wizards** while they are within 3" of the bearer. In addition, add 1 to wound rolls for attacks made by the bearer if the target is a **Wizard** or **Priest**.

CABALISTS

Though they may be barbarous and cruel-hearted, not all Slaves to Darkness are simple reavers. Some of the more magically gifted amongst their number plunge into the ancient study of blood-magic, and through ritual offerings to their insidious gods they seek to bind the power of the aether itself to their will.

Unlike most Slaves to Darkness Hordes, the armies of the Cabalists are dominated by potent sorcerers and mysterious shamans. The power wielded by these warlocks and hex-weavers is held in awe by the tribes that serve them, but it is never enough to satisfy the sorcerers themselves. Their sole desire is to amass greater magical might, for it is through this method that they seek to achieve dark apotheosis. To power their spellcraft, the Cabalists have turned to all manner of disturbing rites and rituals. The majority involve the spilling of blood. Worshippers of all aspects of Chaos can be found in a Cabalist Horde. Even those who view magic with scorn may occasionally pledge their blades to an especially powerful sorcerer, though only in small number and always grudgingly. Cabalist armies consist of deadly warlocks and hard-bitten killers, alongside throngs of lesser tribesmen doomed to provide their blood to fuel the dark spellcraft of the covens' masters. Not all of this blood is given willingly; often those chosen for sacrifice must be restrained by warriors seeking to share in the power of the Cabalists, or even magically controlled by the sorcerers themselves. The prize, however, is considerable. Through their sacrificial arts the Cabalists find their command of the arcane vastly improved; the spells that they muster become almost unstoppable, particularly when many sorcerers work in concert, and even the endless spells that now cross the realms can be temporarily bound to a powerful Cabalist's will.

BATTLE TRAITS – BLOOD SORCERY AND BLACK RITUALS

BINDING RITUALS

The sorcerers of the Cabalists are well versed in the art of blood magic. Through rites of sacrifice and ritual slaughter they seek to draw the power of Chaos to themselves – and the blood of 'willing' allies is the most precious offering of all.

At the start of your hero phase, you can pick 1 friendly **CABALISTS WIZARD** to perform 1 of the following binding rituals:

Ritual of Sorcerous Might: *Calling upon the dark bargains and daemonic pacts they have made, the sorcerers of the Cabalists exchange the lives of their servants for greater magical power.*

Pick 1 friendly **CABALISTS** unit within 3" of the **WIZARD** performing this binding ritual and roll a dice. On a 3+, the ritual is successful and D3 models from that unit are slain. For each model that was slain by this ritual, add 1 to casting rolls made for friendly **CABALISTS WIZARDS** until the end of that phase.

Ritual of Corruption: *Through spilling the lifeblood of their followers, the Cabalists can corrupt the energies of nearby predatory spells and turn them to their own ends, if only for a brief while.*

Pick 1 friendly **CABALISTS** unit within 3" of the **WIZARD** performing this binding ritual and roll a dice. On a 3+, the ritual is successful and D3 models from that unit are slain. Then, pick 1 predatory endless spell within 12" of that **WIZARD**. If 1 model was slain by this ritual, you can move that endless spell up to 3". If 2 models were slain by this ritual, you can move that endless spell up to 6". If 3 models were slain by this ritual, you can move that endless spell up to 9".

MAGIC

CABALISTS WIZARDS know the following spell in addition to any others that they know:

Crippling Ruin: *The caster unleashes a furious barrage of spiteful energy, tearing at their enemies' souls and forcing them to their knees in agony.*

Crippling Ruin has a casting value of 7. If successfully cast, pick 1 enemy unit within 18" of the caster and visible to them. That unit suffers D3 mortal wounds. In addition, reduce the Move characteristic of that unit by the number of mortal wounds inflicted by this spell until your next hero phase.

COMMAND TRAITS – MASTERS OF DARK SORCERY
Cabalists Wizard Hero general only.

D6 Command Trait

1 Bolstered by Hate: *This general is imbued with an unnatural loathing that manifests as a vile nimbus of Chaos energy.*

Add 2 to this general's Wounds characteristic.

2 Lord of Terror: *Where this champion walks, daemonic howls follow them, striking horror into the hearts of all in their path.*

Subtract 1 from the Bravery characteristic of enemy units while they are within 6" of this general.

3 Favoured of the Pantheon: *The gods watch this warlord's deeds particularly closely.*

You can add or subtract 2 from the result of any rolls made for this general on the Eye of the Gods table (pg 68).

4 Mighty Ritualist: *This sorcerous is well versed in the esoteric nuances of sacrificial rituals.*

When this general attempts to perform a Ritual of Sorcerous Might, that ritual is successful on a 2+.

5 Blasphemous Influence: *Even the wildest sorceries are bound by this general's rituals.*

When this general attempts to perform a Ritual of Corruption, that ritual is successful on a 2+.

6 All for One: *This general will sacrifice his pawns for personal gain without hesitation.*

Once per battle, when this general successfully performs a binding ritual, for each model slain by that ritual you can heal 1 wound allocated to this general.

ARTEFACTS OF POWER – CHAOS ESOTERICA
Cabalists Hero only.

D6 Artefact

1 Soul Feeder: *This cursed blade bolsters whoever feeds its endless hunger for souls.*

Pick 1 of the bearer's melee weapons. If the unmodified wound roll for an attack made by that weapon is 6, you can heal 1 wound allocated to the bearer.

2 Black Athame: *This deceptively simple blade has been the instrument of countless bloody sacrifices over the centuries.*

Once per battle, when the bearer attempts to perform a binding ritual, you can say that they will use this artefact. If you do so, that binding ritual is successful (do not roll the dice).

3 Infernal Puppet: *As it dances jerkily upon the aetheric winds, this eldritch marionette violently disrupts the spellcraft of enemy mages.*

Once per battle, in your hero phase, you can pick 1 enemy **Wizard** within 24" of the bearer and visible to them. In the next enemy hero phase, each time that **Wizard** attempts to cast a spell they suffer D3 mortal wounds before the casting roll is made. If the **Wizard** is slain by these mortal wounds, the casting attempt fails (do not roll the dice).

4 Spelleater Pendant: *This star-shaped pendant is carved with sigils of sorcerous deadening. When brandished, it can sap the strength from all but the most powerful incantations.*

The bearer gains the **Wizard** keyword and can attempt to unbind 1 spell in each enemy hero phase. If the bearer is already a **Wizard**, they can attempt to unbind 1 extra spell in each enemy hero phase.

5 Scroll of Dark Unravelling: *When the words scrawled in daemonic gore across this ragged parchment are spoken aloud, even the greatest arcane tempests are soon snuffed out.*

Once per battle, when the bearer attempts to unbind a spell, instead of making an unbinding roll you can say the bearer will use this artefact. If you do so, the spell is automatically unbound (do not roll the dice).

6 Spell Familiar: *This impish daemon has memorised a single spell on behalf of its master, and waits for the moment its knowledge is called upon.*

The bearer knows 1 extra spell from the Lore of the Damned (pg 69).

DESPOILERS

Chosen by their god to receive the ultimate reward, the Daemon Princes of the Despoilers consider it their unholy mission to spread corruption across the realms. At their side march elite warbands of the most powerful Slaves to Darkness, as well as hideously mutated beasts drawn to the dark aura exuded by these damned champions.

To face the Despoilers in battle is to make war against an army of nightmares. The Daemon Princes that lead them, fell beings steeped in age-old malice and the infernal power of the gods, desire nothing less than the ruination of all that could be considered holy or righteous. Whether they alone rule their followers as a pitiless daemonic overlord, or several Princes contest for dominance in the name of their god, the very presence of these beings sees their dark designs brought to fruition. Each is a conduit for the power of Chaos, and where they tread the land rebels. Great crevasses open up in the bedrock of the realms as trees crack and splinter, flaming fissures yawning open in mountainsides from which issue burning torrents of witchfire. Yet most sinister

of all are the thick carpets of darkness that follow the Despoilers, the very light of Hysh swallowed by their unclean presence. This blackness serves the monstrous beings and elite warriors that attend to the most powerful Daemon Princes well; under its obscuring cover, they charge into the enemy with murderous desire filling their souls. The warbands that follow a Despoilers lord will all share the allegiance of the ruling Daemon Prince, and many will be counted amongst the devoted Godtouched; with the power of the Dark Gods flowing through them, they are capable of tearing apart armies many times their size, their unstoppable path of destruction seeing the very realms remade in an image far more pleasing to the insidious nature of pure Chaos.

BATTLE TRAITS – CORRUPTORS OF THE REALMS

SACRILEGIOUS MIGHT

The daemonic warlords of the Despoilers are walking archangels of ruin, and their connection to the power of Chaos makes them incredibly difficult to slay.

Friendly units with the same Mark of Chaos keyword as your general are affected by your general's Aura of Chaos ability while they are wholly within 18" of your general.

In addition, roll a dice each time you allocate a wound or mortal wound to a **DESPOILERS DAEMON PRINCE** that is a general. On a 5+, that wound or mortal wound is negated.

BLESSED BY THE UNHOLY

The monstrous beings of a Despoiler Horde are fortified by the ruinous energies they spread, torn flesh and shattered bones reknitting with terrifying speed.

In your hero phase, you can roll a dice for each friendly **DESPOILERS DAEMON PRINCE** and friendly **DESPOILERS MONSTER** on the battlefield. On a 4+, you can heal up to D3 wounds that have been allocated to that model. If that unit is a **MUTALITH VORTEX BEAST**, you can only heal 1 wound instead of D3.

TWISTED DOMINION

Where a Daemon Prince of the Despoilers walks, chasms open as the land cracks asunder in agonised protest, while thick palls of dark energy obscure the favoured and their servants from view.

If a friendly **DESPOILERS DAEMON PRINCE** finishes a move within 6" of a terrain feature, you can give that terrain feature the Pitch-black and Nightmare Chasm scenery rules below, until your next hero phase. **DESPOILERS DAEMON PRINCES** and **DESPOILERS MONSTERS** are unaffected by these scenery rules.

Pitch-black: Models are not visible to each other if an imaginary straight line 1mm wide drawn between the closest points of the two models crosses over more than 1" of this terrain feature.

Nightmare Chasm: At the start of each hero phase, roll a dice for this terrain feature. On a 6, each unit within 1" of it suffers D3 mortal wounds (roll separately for each unit).

COMMAND TRAITS – ASPECTS OF THE ASCENDED
DESPOILERS DAEMON PRINCE general only.

D6 Command Trait

1 Bolstered by Hate: *This general is imbued with an unnatural loathing that manifests as a crackling corona of Chaos energy.*

Add 2 to this general's Wounds characteristic.

2 Lord of Terror: *Where this champion walks, the inhuman howls of daemonic entities follow them, striking horror into the hearts of all in their path.*

Subtract 1 from the Bravery characteristic of enemy units while they are within 6" of this general.

3 Lightning Reflexes: *The inhuman swiftness of this warlord sees them dart aside from incoming missiles with blinding speed.*

Subtract 1 from hit rolls for attacks made with missile weapons that target this general.

4 Radiance of Dark Glory: *In the presence of this daemon, the mutative energies of Chaos can seal shut even the most grievous of wounds.*

In your hero phase, you can pick 1 friendly **DESPOILERS** unit wholly within 18" of this general and roll a dice. On a 3+, you can heal up to D3 wounds allocated to that unit.

5 Distorting Miasma: *The taint of Chaos spreads from this general with each step they take.*

You can give a terrain feature the Pitch-black and Nightmare Chasm scenery rules (pg 74) if this general finishes a move within 9" of it.

6 Paragon of Ruin: *This general is a living conduit for the will of their patron.*

After set-up is complete but before the first battle round begins, D3 friendly **DESPOILERS** units can move up to 5".

ARTEFACTS OF POWER – INFERNAL TREASURES
DESPOILERS HERO only.

D6 Artefact

1 Crown of Hellish Adoration: *As the wearer's name is chanted in praise, the runes of this twisted diadem form a protective aura around the wearer that can ward off even a cannonball.*

Subtract 1 from wound rolls for attacks made with missile weapons that target the bearer while they are within 3" of any friendly **DESPOILERS** units with at least 3 models.

2 Helm of Many Eyes: *The eyeballs that cover this helm stare into past and future alike, allowing the wearer to catch their foes off guard.*

The bearer and their mount (if they have one) fight at the start of the combat phase if they charged in the same turn, but cannot fight again in that phase unless an ability or spell allows them to fight more than once.

3 Armour of Tortured Souls: *The blackened plates of this armour are strengthened by the souls of its previous wearers, and can withstand all but the most brutal punishment.*

Worsen the Rend characteristic of attacks that target the bearer by 1 (to a minimum of '-').

4 Diabolic Mantle: *The touch of Chaos rests heavily on this warrior's shoulders, providing them with a font of darkling inspiration.*

At the start of the first battle round, if the bearer is on the battlefield, you receive D3 command points.

5 Doombringer Blade: *When this cruel blade is pointed at a hated foe, searing visions pain the bearer's minions until the target has been slain.*

At the start of the first battle round, after set-up is complete but before the first turn begins, you can pick 1 enemy **HERO** or enemy **MONSTER** on the battlefield. If you do so, friendly **DESPOILERS** units can re-roll hit and wound rolls for attacks that target that unit.

6 Realmwarper's Twist-rune: *One who bears this cursed rune upon their flesh can bind warped landscapes to their will.*

Friendly **DESPOILERS** units wholly within 12" of the bearer are unaffected by the Pitch-black and Nightmare Chasm scenery rules.

HOST OF THE EVERCHOSEN

Should a battle require Archaon's personal attention, then he shall bring with him all the might of his dread hosts. These are the conquering armies of the Everchosen, their blades wetted in the blood of a thousand slain empires. Under the command of their dark lord they storm across the field, slaughtering his foes with merciless efficiency.

The most infamous of all Archaon's warriors are the legendary Varanguard. A handful of the Knights of Ruin can turn the tide of any battle, but when the forces of one of the Eight Circles ride out in force there is little that can hope to stand against them and expect to see the next dawn. On occasion the Varanguard alone will be entrusted with ensuring that Archaon's will is done, though just as often they may be joined by throngs of Slaves to Darkness bearing the mark of the Everchosen and who have sworn to serve him above all others. These hosts are deadly enough even when only a few Varanguard are present – and should Archaon himself take to the field, then the doom of the foe is only a matter of time. The Exalted Grand Marshal of the Apocalypse directs his army with a consummate ease, his raw authority mixed with a mastery of tactics and strategy that turns the hordes of Chaos into a more fearsome force than ever. With the treasures of Chaos at his command, most importantly the far-seeing Eye of Sheerian and the monstrous abomination known as Dorghar, Archaon is more than capable of dealing horrific amounts of death himself. The Everchosen is a skilled warrior and powerful wizard, able to dominate and humble any foe foolish enough to lock blades with him. With his Varanguard at his side and the power of the Chaos Gods united behind him, Archaon will not stop his dark crusade until all of the Mortal Realms belong to him, and the Pantheon of Order lies broken at his feet.

BATTLE TRAITS – THE IRON FIST OF THE EVERCHOSEN

EXALTED GRAND MARSHAL OF THE APOCALYPSE

Archaon is the ultimate Champion of Chaos, and by his mere presence does he empower the worshippers of the Dark Gods.

If **ARCHAON** is your general and on the battlefield, friendly **HOST OF THE EVERCHOSEN** units are affected by his Aura of Chaos ability if they are wholly within 18" of him.

FEARLESS IN HIS PRESENCE

None dare flee under Archaon's gaze, for his warriors fear him more than the blades or spells of any foe.

Do not take battleshock tests for friendly **HOST OF THE EVERCHOSEN** units if **ARCHAON** is your general and on the battlefield.

THE WILL OF THE EVERCHOSEN

Nothing will stop the hordes of the Everchosen from destroying those marked for death by Archaon.

In your hero phase, if **ARCHAON** is your general and on the battlefield, you can pick 1 enemy unit on the battlefield. If you do so, you can re-roll hit and wound rolls of 1 for attacks made with melee weapons by friendly **HOST OF THE EVERCHOSEN** units that target that unit until your next hero phase.

COMMAND ABILITY

Dark Prophecy: *With the foresight granted by the Eye of Sheerian, Archaon can adapt his strategies to the flow of the battle and always stay a step ahead of his opponents.*

You can use this command ability at the start of your hero phase if **ARCHAON** is your general and on the battlefield. If you do so, roll a dice and keep the result hidden from your opponent. At the start of the next battle round, before players determine who has the first turn, you can reveal the result. On a 1-3 your opponent must take the first turn of that battle round. On a 4-6 you must take the first turn of that battle round.

THE EIGHT CIRCLES OF THE VARANGUARD

Archaon charges each of his would-be champions with eight trials in the ultimate test of their mettle. Those skilled enough to triumph are placed into one of the infamous Eight Circles of the Varanguard.

After you have given the **HOST OF THE EVERCHOSEN** keyword to your army, you must choose one of the keywords from the list below. All **VARANGUARD** units in your army gain that keyword.

FIRST CIRCLE, **SECOND CIRCLE**, **THIRD CIRCLE**, **FOURTH CIRCLE**, **FIFTH CIRCLE**, **SIXTH CIRCLE**, **SEVENTH CIRCLE** or **EIGHTH CIRCLE**.

THE FIRST CIRCLE

The Swords of Chaos: *Descending from ruinous portals torn open in the sky, the attacks of the Swords of Chaos are almost impossible to predict before it is too late.*

At the start of the first battle round, after determining who has the first turn, you can remove any friendly **FIRST CIRCLE** units from the battlefield and set them up again (any restrictions in the set-up instructions for the battleplan being used still apply).

THE SECOND CIRCLE

The Souls of Torment: *Sowers of sorrow and despair, the Varanguard of the Second Circle grant their foes the release of death only when all hope is lost.*

Subtract 1 from the Bravery characteristic of enemy units while they are within 6" of any friendly **SECOND CIRCLE** units. In addition, if an enemy unit fails a battleshock test within 6" of any friendly **SECOND CIRCLE** units, add D3 to the number of models that flee.

THE THIRD CIRCLE

The Scions of Darkness: *These dreaded warriors are cloaked in unnatural shadow, confounding the aim of those who would seek to bring them down from afar.*

Subtract 1 from hit rolls for attacks made with missile weapons that target **THIRD CIRCLE** units.

THE FOURTH CIRCLE

The Reavers of Chaos: *Desolation is all that is left in the wake of the Fourth Circle. The very lands they pass through are filled with the dark power of Chaos, and furiously lash out at the enemies of the gods.*

In your hero phase, you can pick 1 terrain feature within 3" of any friendly **FOURTH CIRCLE** units. Each enemy unit within 3" of that terrain features suffers D3 mortal wounds (roll separately for each unit).

THE FIFTH CIRCLE

The Scourges of Fate: *The Varanguard of the Fifth Circle are Archaon's headhunters. Even the greatest of heroes and most fearsome of monsters cannot escape their blades for long.*

You can re-roll hit and wound rolls for attacks made by **FIFTH CIRCLE** units if the target is a **HERO** or **MONSTER**.

THE SIXTH CIRCLE

The Blades of Desolation: *Where the Sixth Circle ride, none can withstand them. They are the hammer of the Everchosen, the weapon he wields when an enemy must be utterly shattered.*

Add 1 to the damage inflicted by attacks made with melee weapons by **SIXTH CIRCLE** units that charged in the same turn.

THE SEVENTH CIRCLE

The Bane Sons: *To consume the flesh of an opponent is to inherit their strength, so claim the cannibal riders of the Bane Sons. They have yet to be proven wrong.*

At the end of the combat phase, if any attacks made by a friendly **SEVENTH CIRCLE** unit in that phase destroyed any enemy units, heal up to D3 wounds allocated to that **SEVENTH CIRCLE** unit.

THE EIGHTH CIRCLE

The Nameless Circle: *Archaon alone knows the true nature of the Eighth Circle, and the only evidence to mark their passing is the broken corpses of their foes.*

EIGHTH CIRCLE units can fly.

BATTLEPLAN
THE THRESHOLD OF DAMNATION

To walk the Path to Glory is to sell one's soul to rapacious gods. The only way to rise higher is to commit ever-increasing acts of evil. Some champions – particularly those of a magical persuasion – draw the eye of the gods through performing of dark rituals. The purpose of such a ritual can vary greatly based on the agenda of the sorcerer, but all demand a heavy price and can wreak untold havoc if successfully brought to completion. Those who stand before the armies of Chaos will stop at nothing to prevent such a ritual coming to pass, for should it be successful their very souls are endangered.

This battleplan allows you to re-create just such a clash. The warbands of a powerful sorcerer have closed in on a site of dark power, and now their magical master seeks to unleash unspeakable evil upon the land. The defenders are all that stands before the sorcerer and their goal, and must strive to destroy the fuel for the sorcerer's rites – their barbarous servants – before the ritual grows too powerful to stop.

THE ARMIES

Each player picks an army as described in the core rules. One player is the Slaves to Darkness player and their opponent is the Desperate Defender. The Slaves to Darkness player's army must have a **Chaos Sorcerer Lord** as its general and include at least 1 unit of 20 **Chaos Marauders** or 10 **Chaos Warriors**.

SET-UP

The territories for both armies are shown on the map. The players alternate setting up units one at a time starting with the Slaves to Darkness player. The Slaves to Darkness player's units must be set up wholly within their territory. The Desperate Defender's units must be set up wholly within their territory.

Continue to set up units until both players have set up their armies. If one player finishes first, the opposing player can set up the rest of the units in their army one after another.

FIRST TURN

The Slaves to Darkness player takes the first turn in the first battle round.

COMMAND ABILITIES

The following additional command abilities can be used in this battle:

Endless Followers: *The armies of Chaos are nearly endless, and for each tribesman who falls there is soon another to take their place.*

The Slaves to Darkness player can use this command ability in their hero phase. If they do so, they can return D3 slain models to each **Chaos Marauders** unit from their army that is wholly within 16" of their general.

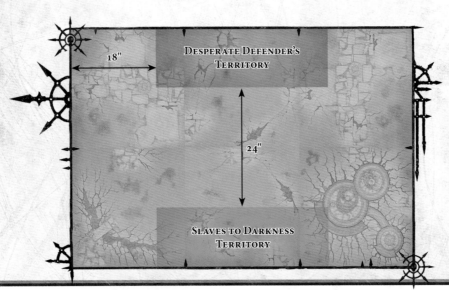

On Me!: *The general of the defenders knows well the cost of failure, and will exhort their warriors to the limits of endurance in order to deny the Slaves to Darkness victory.*

The Desperate Defender can use this command ability at the start of their hero phase. If they do so, they can pick 1 unit from their army wholly within 16" of their general. That unit can run and still charge later in the same turn.

THE RITUAL

The sorcerers of the Slaves to Darkness will not hesitate to sacrifice their minions in the pursuit of power, for only one willing to commit any evil in the name of the gods can hope to achieve daemonhood.

At the start of their hero phase, the Slaves to Darkness player can pick 1 **SLAVES TO DARKNESS** unit

from their army wholly within 12" of their general. If they do so, D3 models from that unit are slain but they add 1 to casting, dispelling and unbinding rolls for **WIZARDS** from their army until their next hero phase.

BATTLE LENGTH

The battle lasts until a player wins a **major victory** or for 5 battle rounds, whichever happens first.

GLORIOUS VICTORY

If 10 or more models from the Slaves to Darkness army are slain as a result of The Ritual ability (see left), the Slaves to Darkness player wins a **major victory**.

If the general of the Slaves to Darkness army is slain, the Desperate Defender wins a **major victory**.

If the Desperate Defender's army is destroyed before the end of the fifth battle round, the Slaves to Darkness player wins a **minor victory**.

If all of the **CHAOS MARAUDERS** units from the Slaves to Darkness army have been destroyed at the end of the battle, the Desperate Defender wins a **minor victory**.

If none of the above conditions have been met at the end of the battle, the game is a **draw**.

PATH TO GLORY

Path to Glory campaigns centre around collecting and fighting a series of battles with a warband in the Mortal Realms. Players start off with a small number of units. Over the course of several battles, each warband will gather more followers to join them in their quest for glory and renown.

In order to take part in a Path to Glory campaign, you will need two or more players. Each player will need a **Hero** to be their champion and must then create a warband to follow and fight beside their champion during the campaign.

The players fight battles against each other using the warbands they have created. The results of these battles will gain their warbands glory. After battle, warbands may swell in numbers as more warriors flock to their banner, or existing troops may become more powerful.

After gaining sufficient glory or growing your warband enough to dominate all others through sheer weight of numbers, you will be granted a final test. Succeed, and you will be crowned the victor of the campaign, your glory affirmed for all time.

CREATING A WARBAND

In a Path to Glory game, you do not select your army in the normal manner. Instead, you create a warband that consists of a mighty champion, battling to earn the favour of the gods, and their followers. The details and progress of each warband need to be recorded on a warband roster, which you can download for free from games-workshop.com.

To create a warband, simply follow these steps and record the results on your warband roster:

1. First, pick a faction for your warband. Each faction has its own set of warband tables that are used to generate the units in the warband and the rewards they can receive for fighting battles. The warband tables included in this battletome let you collect a Slaves to Darkness warband, but other Warhammer Age of Sigmar publications include warband tables to let you collect warbands from other factions.

2. Next, choose your warband's champion by selecting one of the options from your faction's champion table. Give your champion a suitably grand name and write this down on your warband roster.

3. Having picked your champion, the next step is to make follower rolls to generate your starting followers. The champion you chose in step 2 will determine how many follower rolls you have. To make a follower roll, pick a column from one of the followers tables and then roll a dice. If you prefer, instead of rolling a dice, you can pick the result from the followers table (this still uses up the roll).

   Sometimes a table will require you to expend two or more rolls, or one roll and a number of Glory Points (see Gaining Glory), in order to use it. Note that the option to expend Glory Points can only be used when you add new followers to your warband after a battle (see Rewards of Battle). In either case, in order to generate a follower unit from the table, you must have enough rolls and/or Glory Points to meet the requirements, and you can then either roll once on the table or pick one result from the table of your choice. If you expend Glory Points, you must reduce your Glory Points total by the amount shown on the table.

   Followers are organised into units. The followers table tells you how many models the unit has. Follower units cannot include additional models, but they can otherwise take any options listed on their warscroll. Record all of the information about your followers on your warband roster.

4. You can use 1 follower roll to allow your champion to start the campaign with a Champion's Reward or to allow 1 of your follower units to start the campaign with a Follower's Reward (see Rewards of Battle).

5. Finally, give your warband a name, one that will inspire respect and dread in your rivals. Your warband is now complete and you can fight your first battle. Good luck!

TO WAR!

Having created a warband, you can now fight battles with it against other warbands taking part in the campaign. You can fight battles as and when you wish, and you can use any of the battleplans available for Warhammer Age of Sigmar. The units you use for a game must be those on your roster.

When you use a Slaves to Darkness warband in a Path to Glory game, you can use the battle traits from pages 67-68. You cannot use any other Slaves to Darkness allegiance abilities.

Any casualties suffered by a warband are assumed to have been replaced in time for its next battle. If your champion is slain in a battle, it is assumed that they were merely injured; they are back to full strength for your next game, thirsty for vengeance!

GAINING GLORY

All of the players in the campaign are vying for glory. The amount of glory they have received is represented by the Glory Points that the warband has accumulated.

As a warband's glory increases, it will also attract additional followers, and a warband's champion may be granted rewards.

Warbands receive Glory Points after a battle is complete. If the warband drew or lost the battle, it receives 1 Glory Point. If it won the battle, it receives D3 Glory Points (re-roll a result of 1 if it won a **major victory**).

Add the Glory Points you scored to the total recorded on your roster. Once you have won 10 Glory Points, you will have a chance to win the campaign (see Eternal Glory).

REWARDS OF BATTLE

After each battle, you can take one of the three following options. Alternatively, roll a D3 to determine which option to take.

D3   Option

1   Additional Followers: *More loyal followers flock to your banner.*

You receive 1 follower roll that can be used to select a new unit from a followers table and add it to your warband roster. See step 3 of Creating a Warband for details of how to use the followers table to add a unit to your warband.

Once 5 new units have joined your warband, you will have a chance to win the campaign (see Eternal Glory).

2   Champion's Reward: *Your champion's prowess grows.*

Roll on your champion rewards table for your warband and note the result on your warband roster. Your champion can only receive one Champion's Reward – if they already have a Champion's Reward, you must take a Follower's Reward instead.

3   Follower's Reward: *Your warriors become renowned for mighty deeds.*

Pick 1 unit of followers and then roll on the followers rewards table for your warband. Note the result on your warband roster. A unit can only receive one Follower's Reward. If all of your follower units have a Follower's Reward, you must take Additional Followers instead.

ETERNAL GLORY

There are two ways to win a Path to Glory campaign: by Blood or by Might. To win by Blood, your warband must first have 10 Glory Points. To win by Might, your warband must have at least 5 additional units of followers. In either case, you must then fight and win one more battle to win the campaign. If the next battle you fight is tied or lost, you do not receive any Glory Points – just keep on fighting battles until you win the campaign… or another player wins first!

You can shorten or lengthen a campaign by lowering or raising the number of Glory Points needed to win by Blood or the number of extra units that must join a warband to win by Might. For example, for a shorter campaign, you could say that a warband only needs 5 Glory Points before the final fight, or for a longer one, you could say that 15 are needed.

SLAVES TO DARKNESS WARBAND TABLES

Use the following tables to determine the champion that leads your warband, the followers that make up the other units in the warband, and the rewards the warband receives after battle.

CHAMPION TABLE

Champion	Follower Rolls
Chaos Lord on Manticore or Chaos Sorcerer Lord on Manticore	2
Chaos Lord on Daemonic Mount or Chaos Lord on Karkadrak	3
Chaos Lord, Chaos Sorcerer Lord or Slaves to Darkness Daemon Prince	4

HERO FOLLOWERS TABLE

D6	Followers
1-2	Exalted Hero of Chaos
3-4	Darkoath Warqueen or Darkoath Chieftain
5-6	Ogroid Myrmidon

RETINUE FOLLOWERS TABLE

3D6	Followers
3-4	Chaos Spawn
5-6	6 Raptoryx or 6 Furies
7-8	18 Unmade or 18 Untamed Beasts
9-10	16 Cypher Lords or 18 Spire Tyrants
11-12	18 Corvus Cabal
13-14	20 Splintered Fang or 16 Iron Golems
15-16	20 Chaos Marauders or 5 Chaos Warriors
17-18	Chaos Chariot or Gorebeast Chariot

EVERCHOSEN RETINUE FOLLOWERS TABLE
(uses 2 rolls, or 1 roll and 1 Glory Point)

D6	Followers
1-6	3 Varanguard

MONSTERS FOLLOWERS TABLE
(uses 2 rolls, or 1 roll and 1 Glory Point)

D6	Followers
1-2	Fomoroid Crusher
3	Mindstealer Sphiranx
4	Mutalith Vortex Beast
5	Slaughterbrute
6	Soul Grinder

ELITE RETINUE FOLLOWERS TABLE
(uses 2 rolls, or 1 roll and 1 Glory Point)

D6	Followers
1	5 Chaos Chosen
2-3	5 Chaos Knights
4-5	10 Chaos Warriors
6	Chaos Warshrine

FOLLOWERS REWARDS TABLE

D3	Reward
1	**Keen for Conflict:** *These warriors are forever eager to get to grips with their enemies.* This unit can run and still charge later in the same turn.
2	**Skilled and Scarred:** *With every battle these warriors develop their deadly skills further.* Add 1 to hit rolls for attacks made by this unit if it charged in the same turn.
3	**Furious Fervour:** *Even impending death cannot prevent these warriors from striking down their foes.* If a model from this unit is slain in the combat phase, it can fight before it is removed from play.

CHAMPION REWARDS TABLE
EYE OF THE GODS HERO only.

D6	Reward
1	**Flames of Spite:** *Chaotic fire clings to the form of this warlord.* If the unmodified wound roll for an attack made by this champion is 6, the target suffers 1 mortal wound in addition to any normal damage.
2-3	**Favoured of the Pantheon:** *The gods watch this warlord's deeds particularly closely.* You can add or subtract 2 from the result of any rolls made for this champion on the Eye of the Gods table (pg 68).
4-5	**Bolstered by Hate:** *This general is imbued with an unnatural loathing that manifests as a vile nimbus of Chaos energy.* Add 1 to this champion's Wounds characteristic.
6	**Artefact of Power:** *An ancient artefact of power has come into this champion's possession.* Randomly generate one artefact of power for this champion from the Trophies of Conquest table (pg 71).

CHAMPION REWARDS TABLE
WIZARD HERO only.

D6	Reward
1	**Studied Sorcerer:** *Mastery of the arcane is of the utmost importance for this wizard.* Add 1 to casting, dispelling and unbinding rolls for this champion.
2-3	**Favoured of the Pantheon:** *The gods watch this warlord's deeds particularly closely.* You can add or subtract 2 from the result of any rolls made for this champion on the Eye of the Gods table (pg 68).
4-5	**Lord of Terror:** *Where this champion walks, the inhuman howls of daemons follow them, striking horror into the hearts of all in their path.* Subtract 1 from the Bravery characteristic of enemy units while they are within 6" of this champion.
6	**Artefact of Power:** *An ancient artefact of power has come into this champion's possession.* Randomly generate one artefact of power for this champion from the Chaos Esoterica table (pg 73).

CHAMPION REWARDS TABLE
DAEMON PRINCE only.

D3	Reward		
1	**Paragon of Ruin:** *This champion is truly favoured by their god, a living conduit for their fell power.* Friendly units are affected by this champion's Aura of Chaos ability while they are wholly within 18" of this champion.	2	**Lightning Reflexes:** *The inhuman swiftness of this warlord sees them dart aside from incoming strikes with blinding speed.* Roll a dice each time you allocate a wound or mortal wound to this champion. On a 5+ that wound or mortal wound is negated.	3	**Artefact of Power:** *An ancient artefact of power has come into this champion's possession.* Randomly generate one artefact of power for this champion from the Infernal Treasures table (pg 75).

WARSCROLLS

This section includes the Slaves to Darkness warscrolls, warscroll battalions and endless spell warscrolls. Updated December 2019; the warscrolls printed here take precedence over any warscrolls with an earlier publication date or no publication date.

WARSCROLL BATTALION
CHAOS HORDE

When a Chaos Horde is on the march, the Mortal Realms tremble. Hundreds of marauding barbarians and armoured warriors cut down all in their path as they roar oaths to the dark pantheon. They revel in slaughter, and the pace with which their battle-hungry armies cover ground can catch even the most astute foe off guard. Ruling over the Horde is a Godsworn Overlord, a formidable champion who has risen high in the gaze of the Chaos Gods and whose commands are followed without question – as long as they can exert their authority.

ORGANISATION

- 1 Godsworn Champions of Ruin

- 4-8 warscroll battalions chosen from the following list in any combination: Godswrath Warband, Ruinbringer Warband, Bloodmarked Warband, Fatesworn Warband, Plaguetouched Warband, Pleasurebound Warband

ABILITIES
Oncoming Onslaught: *Rallied under the banner of their overlord, a Chaos Horde on the warpath is all but unstoppable.*

Once per turn, you can use 1 command ability on the warscroll of a **HERO** from this battalion without a command point being spent. In addition, add 2" to the Move characteristic of units from this battalion in the first battle round.

WARSCROLL BATTALION
GODSWORN CHAMPIONS OF RUIN

ORGANISATION

- 1 unit chosen from the following list: **Chaos Lord**, **Chaos Sorcerer Lord**, Exalted Hero of Chaos, Ogroid Myrmidon, Slaves to Darkness Daemon Prince, Darkoath Warqueen, Darkoath Chieftain

- 4-8 units chosen in any combination from the following list: Chaos Chosen, Chaos Knights, Chaos Warriors, Chaos Marauders, Chaos Marauder Horsemen

ABILITIES

Fury of the Damned: *The lords of the Slaves to Darkness are always seeking to prove their might before the gods, pushing themselves to new and terrifying feats of slaughter.*

In your hero phase, you can pick 1 **Hero** from this battalion that is within 3" of an enemy unit. If you do so, that **Hero** can fight.

WARSCROLL BATTALION
GODSWRATH WARBAND

ORGANISATION

- 1 unit chosen from the following list: Chaos Lord on Manticore, Chaos Sorcerer Lord on Manticore, Chaos Lord on Daemonic Mount, Chaos Lord on Karkadrak, Chaos Lord or Chaos Sorcerer Lord

- 4-8 units chosen in any combination from the following list: Chaos Chosen, Chaos Knights, Chaos Warriors, Chaos Marauders, Chaos Marauder Horsemen

- 1 or more Chaos Warshrines

ABILITIES

Searing Doombolts: *Empowered by chanting apostles, the Warshrine unleashes bolts of hellish energies.*

In your hero phase, you can pick 1 **Chaos Warshrine** from this battalion and roll a dice for each enemy unit within 24" of that **Chaos Warshrine** and visible to it. For each 6, that unit suffers D3 mortal wounds.

WARSCROLL BATTALION
RUINBRINGER WARBAND

ORGANISATION

- 1 unit chosen from the following list: Chaos Lord on Daemonic Mount, Chaos Lord on Karkadrak

- 4-8 units chosen in any combination from the following list: Chaos Knights, Chaos Chariots, Gorebeast Chariots, Chaos Marauder Horsemen

ABILITIES

Dark Cavalry: *The charge of a Ruinbringer Warband can sweep away entire enemy formations.*

Each time a unit from this battalion finishes a charge move, you can pick 1 enemy unit within 1" of that unit. If you do so, roll a dice. On a 2+, that enemy unit suffers D3 mortal wounds.

WARSCROLL BATTALION
BLOODMARKED WARBAND

ORGANISATION

- 1 Mortal Slaves to Darkness Khorne Hero

- 8 Mortal Slaves to Darkness Khorne units

This warscroll battalion is part of the Khorne faction and the Slaves to Darkness faction.

ABILITIES

Blood Rage: *As a Khornate lord kills, waves of bloodlust wash over his comrades, filling them with an unstoppable fury that can only be satiated by slaughter.*

If a **Hero** from this battalion slays any enemy models in the combat phase, you can pick 1 unit from the same battalion wholly within 12" of that **Hero**. Add 1 to the Attacks characteristic of that unit's melee weapons until your next hero phase. The same unit cannot benefit from this ability more than once per battle round.

WARSCROLL BATTALION
FATESWORN WARBAND

ORGANISATION

- 1 Mortal Slaves to Darkness Tzeentch Hero

- 9 Mortal Slaves to Darkness Tzeentch units

This warscroll battalion is part of the Tzeentch faction and the Slaves to Darkness faction.

ABILITIES

Scions of Change: *Tzeentch's sacred number is nine; fortune favours those of his followers who adhere to it.*

At the start of your hero phase, you can pick 1 unit from this battalion that has 9 or more models. If you do so, until the end of that phase, that unit can attempt to cast 1 spell and attempt to dispel 1 endless spell. It knows the Stolen Sting spell:

Stolen Sting: *With a garbled cascade of change-incantations, the caster warps and blunts the enemy's blades.*

Stolen Sting has a casting value of 7. If successfully cast, pick 1 enemy unit within 18" of the caster and visible to them. Worsen the Rend characteristic of that unit's melee weapons by 1 until your next hero phase. A unit cannot be affected by this spell more than once per turn.

WARSCROLL BATTALION
PLAGUETOUCHED WARBAND

ORGANISATION

- 1 Mortal Slaves to Darkness Nurgle Hero

- 7 Mortal Slaves to Darkness Nurgle units

This warscroll battalion is part of the Nurgle faction and the Slaves to Darkness faction.

ABILITIES

Grandfather's Favour: *The blessings of the Plague God prime these warriors with bile-swollen physiques that are ready to explode in torrents of foulness when struck.*

If the unmodified wound roll for an attack made with a melee weapon that targets a unit from this battalion is 6, the attacking unit suffers 1 mortal wound after all of its attacks have been resolved. In addition, in your hero phase, you can pick 1 unit from this battalion and 1 enemy unit within 1" of it. If you do so, roll a dice. On a 3+, that enemy unit suffers D3 mortal wounds.

WARSCROLL BATTALION
PLEASUREBOUND WARBAND

ORGANISATION

- 1 MORTAL SLAVES TO DARKNESS SLAANESH HERO

- 6 MORTAL SLAVES TO DARKNESS SLAANESH units

This warscroll battalion is part of the Slaanesh faction and the Slaves to Darkness faction.

ABILITIES

Perverse Yearnings: *The sight of inflicted torment sees these decadent warriors surge forth, eager to give and receive the gift of agony.*

If a model from this battalion is slain in the combat phase, units from the same battalion can move an extra 3" when they pile in until your next hero phase.

WARSCROLL BATTALION
OVERLORDS OF CHAOS

ORGANISATION

- 3-6 HOST OF THE EVERCHOSEN VARANGUARD units

ABILITIES

The Circles Unleashed: *When Archaon has marked a specific foe for destruction, he will call to his side those of the Varanguard best suited to the task.*

When you select this battalion to be part of your army, you can give each unit in this battalion one of the following keywords: FIRST CIRCLE, SECOND CIRCLE, THIRD CIRCLE, FOURTH CIRCLE, FIFTH CIRCLE, SIXTH CIRCLE, SEVENTH CIRCLE or EIGHTH CIRCLE.

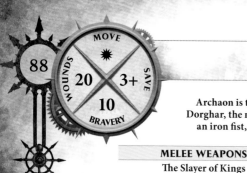

ARCHAON
THE EVERCHOSEN

MOVE						
20	**3+**					
10						
WOUNDS	**SAVE**					
BRAVERY						

Archaon is the Everchosen, the favoured warlord of the dark pantheon. From atop Dorghar, the monstrous Steed of the Apocalypse, Archaon commands his legions with an iron fist, his deadly skill and unholy powers sealing the doom of entire armies.

MELEE WEAPONS	Range	Attacks	To Hit	To Wound	Rend	Damage
The Slayer of Kings	1"	4	2+	3+	-2	3
Monstrous Claws	1"	2	2+	3+	-2	D6
Lashing Tails	3"	2D6	4+	3+	-	1
Three Heads	3"	✲	3+	3+	-1	2

DAMAGE TABLE		
Wounds Suffered	Move	Three Heads
0-4	14"	6
5-8	12"	5
9-12	10"	4
13-15	8"	3
16+	6"	2

DESCRIPTION

Archaon is a named character that is a single model. He is armed with the Slayer of Kings.

FLY: This model can fly.

MOUNT: Dorghar attacks with his Monstrous Claws, Lashing Tails and Three Heads.

ABILITIES

The Armour of Morkar: *Archaon's armour is inscribed with powerful sigils of warding.*

Roll a dice each time you allocate a mortal wound to this model. On a 1-3 nothing happens. On a 4-5, that mortal wound is negated. On a 6, that mortal wound is negated and the attacking unit suffers 1 mortal wound.

The Crown of Domination: *This forbidding helm exudes a palpable aura of menace.*

Add 2 to the Bravery characteristic of friendly **CHAOS** units wholly within 12" of this model. In addition, subtract 2 from the Bravery characteristic of enemy units while they are within 12" of this model.

The Eye of Sheerian: *Ripped from the corpse of the Chaos Dragon Flamefang, this ancient treasure forewarns Archaon of events yet to pass.*

Re-roll hit rolls of 6 for attacks made by enemy units that target this model.

The Everchosen: *The Ruinous Powers shelter their champion from hostile enemy magics.*

Each time this model is affected by a spell or endless spell, you can roll a dice. If you do so, on a 4+, ignore the effects of that spell or endless spell on this model.

The Slayer of Kings: *This ancient daemonblade thirsts for the souls of champions and warlords.*

If the unmodified wound roll for 2 attacks that target the same enemy **HERO** in the same phase with the Slayer of Kings is 6, that **HERO** is slain.

Three-headed Titan: *The greater daemons consumed by Dorghar imbue the steed with unlimited power.*

At the start of your hero phase, you can say that Dorghar will draw upon his daemonic might. If you do so, choose 1 of the following effects:

Filth-spewer: *Dorghar's Nurglesque head vomits a cascade of half-digested warriors and bile.*

Pick 1 enemy unit within 12" of this model and roll a dice. On a 3+, that unit suffers D3 mortal wounds.

Skull-gorger: *Dorghar's Khornate head devours the skulls of prey to invigorate his master.*

You can heal up to D3 wounds allocated to this model.

Spell-eater: *Dorghar's Tzeentchian head consumes eldritch energies from nearby spells.*

Pick 1 endless spell within 18" of this model; that endless spell is dispelled.

Warlord Without Equal: *Archaon's mastery of war is near unparalleled, and under his command the Slaves to Darkness are an unstoppable force.*

If this model is on the battlefield at the start of your hero phase, you receive 1 extra command point.

MAGIC

Archaon is a **WIZARD**. He can attempt to cast 2 spells in your hero phase and attempt to unbind 2 spells in the enemy hero phase. He knows the Arcane Bolt and Mystic Shield spells.

COMMAND ABILITIES

By My Will: *All Slaves to Darkness recognise Archaon's supreme authority, and fear his wrath more than any foe should they fail him.*

You can use this command ability once per turn in the hero phase. If you do so, pick 1 friendly **SLAVES TO DARKNESS** unit on the battlefield. Until the end of the battle round, if a model from that unit is slain by an attack made with a melee weapon, that model can fight before it is removed from play.

All-seeing Dominion: *The Eye of Sheerian grants Archaon foreknowledge of the flow of battle. Enemies who place their hopes in a single tactical master stroke find themselves confounded when their efforts are met with the perfect counter.*

You can use this command ability when your opponent spends a command point. If you do so, roll a dice before resolving the effects of any command ability that command point is spent on. On a 1, this command ability has no effect. On a 2+, this model can use the By My Will command ability above without a command point being spent, even if it is not the hero phase and even if that command ability has already been used in the same turn.

KEYWORDS	CHAOS, DAEMON, MORTAL, SLAVES TO DARKNESS, EVERCHOSEN, KHORNE, TZEENTCH, NURGLE, SLAANESH, HEDONITE, UNDIVIDED, MONSTER, HERO, WIZARD, ARCHAON

VARANGUARD

MOVE 10"
WOUNDS 5
SAVE 3+
BRAVERY 9

Each of the Varanguard is a mighty champion who has passed the many tests set for them by Archaon and sworn themselves to his service. Riding atop their hulking steeds, these lords of darkness bring inescapable death to the Everchosen's enemies.

MELEE WEAPONS	Range	Attacks	To Hit	To Wound	Rend	Damage
Ensorcelled Weapon	1"	6	3+	3+	-1	1
Fellspear	2"	3	3+	4+	-1	2
Daemonforged Blade	1"	3	3+	3+	-1	D3
Tearing Fangs	1"	3	4+	3+	-	1

DESCRIPTION

A unit of Varanguard has any number of models, each armed with one of the following weapon options: Ensorcelled Weapon; Fellspear; or Daemonforged Blade.

MOUNT: This unit's Mutated Steeds attack with their Tearing Fangs.

MARK OF CHAOS: When you select this unit to be part of your army, you must give it one of the following Mark of Chaos keywords: **Khorne**, **Nurgle**, **Slaanesh**, **Tzeentch** or **Undivided**.

ABILITIES

Daemonbound: *Weapons that contain the essence of a daemon are capable of swiftly devouring an enemy's soul.*

If the unmodified hit roll for an attack made with a Daemonforged Blade is 6, that attack inflicts 1 mortal wound on the target in addition to any normal damage.

Favoured of the Everchosen: *When the Varanguard ride to war alongside their dark master they are truly formidable.*

Add 1 to hit rolls for attacks made with melee weapons by this unit (excluding those of its mounts) if **Archaon** is in your army and on the battlefield.

Impaling Charge: *Varanguard armed with Fellspears are utterly deadly on the charge, their weapons lowered to skewer the enemy upon their vicious points.*

Add 1 to wound rolls for attacks made with this unit's Fellspears and improve the Rend characteristic of this unit's Fellspears by 1 if it made a charge move in the same turn.

Relentless Killers: *The Varanguard have slaughtered foes beyond counting, butchering their way across the battlefields of the Mortal Realms without mercy.*

Once per battle, in the combat phase, after this unit has fought in that phase for the first time, when it is your turn to pick a unit to fight, this unit can be picked to fight for a second time if it is within 3" of any enemy units.

Warpsteel Shields: *The great shields carried by the Varanguard provide protection against even the most potent magical attacks.*

Each time this unit is affected by a spell or endless spell, you can roll a dice. If you do so, on a 5+, ignore the effects of that spell or endless spell on this unit.

KEYWORDS CHAOS, MORTAL, SLAVES TO DARKNESS, EVERCHOSEN, MARK OF CHAOS, VARANGUARD

GAUNT SUMMONER
ON DISC OF TZEENTCH

MOVE	16"
WOUNDS	6
SAVE	6+
BRAVERY	8

90

The Gaunt Summoners are strange daemon-sorcerers of Tzeentch bound to the will of the Everchosen. They glide above the battlefield on scintillating Discs of Tzeentch, laying the enemy low with arcane power and cursed daggers.

MISSILE WEAPONS	Range	Attacks	To Hit	To Wound	Rend	Damage
Changestaff	18"	1	3+	4+	-	D3
MELEE WEAPONS	Range	Attacks	To Hit	To Wound	Rend	Damage
Warptongue Blade	1"	1	3+	4+	-	1
Blades and Stingers	1"	D3	4+	4+	-	1

DESCRIPTION

A Gaunt Summoner on Disc of Tzeentch is a single model armed with a Changestaff and Warptongue Blade.

FLY: This model can fly.

MOUNT: This model's Disc of Tzeentch attacks with its Blades and Stingers.

ABILITIES

Book of Profane Secrets: *Whispering fell incantations, a Gaunt Summoner can temporarily divert the path of a Realmgate, allowing malefic Chaos entities to manifest on the battlefield.*

Once per battle, at the start of your hero phase, you can say this model will use its Book of Profane Secrets. If you do so, you can summon 1 unit from the list below to the battlefield, and add it to your army, but the number of spells that this model can attempt to cast in that phase is reduced by 1. The summoned unit must be set up wholly within 9" of this model and more than 9" from any enemy units.

Choose 1 unit from the following list:

• 10 Pink Horrors
• 10 Bloodletters
• 10 Plaguebearers
• 10 Daemonettes
• 6 Furies

Hovering Disc of Tzeentch: *A Gaunt Summoner mounted on a Disc of Tzeentch is capable of truly breathtaking feats of agility and evasion.*

Add 2 to save rolls for attacks made with melee weapons that target this model unless the attacking unit is a **MONSTER** or can fly.

Warptongue Blade: *Those cut by a Warptongue Blade soon find their bodies wracked with sickening and uncontrollable mutations.*

If the unmodified wound roll for an attack made with a Warptongue Blade is 6, that attacks inflicts D6 mortal wounds on the target and the attack sequence ends (do not make a save roll).

MAGIC

This model is a **WIZARD**. It can attempt to cast 2 spells in your hero phase and attempt to unbind 2 spells in the enemy hero phase. It knows the Arcane Bolt, Mystic Shield and Infernal Flames spells.

Infernal Flames: *The Gaunt Summoner conjures a rolling wave of scorching wyrdfire that engulfs enemy formations.*

Infernal Flames has a casting value of 7. If successfully cast, pick 1 enemy unit within 12" of the caster and visible to them, and roll 1 dice for each model in that unit. For each 5+, that unit suffers 1 mortal wound. If that unit is a **MONSTER** or **WAR MACHINE**, roll 3 dice for each model instead.

KEYWORDS	CHAOS, DAEMON, MORTAL, SLAVES TO DARKNESS, EVERCHOSEN, TZEENTCH, HERO, WIZARD, GAUNT SUMMONER

CHAOS LORD
ON MANTICORE

91

With raw strength and force of will, the greatest Chaos Lords seek to claim a ferocious Manticore as a mount. Those who succeed find their killing power greatly amplified, and are amongst the deadliest champions of the Ruinous Powers.

MELEE WEAPONS	Range	Attacks	To Hit	To Wound	Rend	Damage
Daemon Blade	1"	3	3+	3+	-1	D3
Chaos Lance	2"	3	3+	3+	-	2
Chaos Flail	2"	6	3+	3+	-	1
Honed Fangs and Claws	1"	5	3+	✱	-1	2
Shredding Tail	3"	✱	4+	4+	-	1

DAMAGE TABLE			
Wounds Suffered	Move	Honed Fangs and Claws	Shredding Tail
0-2	12"	1+	5
3-4	10"	2+	4
5-7	8"	3+	3
8-9	6"	4+	2
10+	6"	5+	1

DESCRIPTION

A Chaos Lord on Manticore is a single model armed with one of the following weapon options: Daemon Blade and Chaos Lance; Chaos Flail and Chaos Lance; Daemon Blade and Chaos Runeshield; Chaos Flail and Chaos Runeshield; Daemon Blade and Daggerfist; or Chaos Flail and Daggerfist.

MOUNT: This model's Manticore attacks with its Honed Fangs and Claws, and Shredding Tail.

FLY: This model can fly.

MARK OF CHAOS: When you select this model to be part of your army, you must give it one of the following Mark of Chaos keywords: KHORNE, TZEENTCH, NURGLE, SLAANESH or UNDIVIDED.

ABILITIES

Chaos Runeshield: *The dark runes inscribed upon these shields grant them the power to withstand even the most powerful attacks.*

Roll a dice each time you allocate a mortal wound to this model. On a 5+, that mortal wound is negated.

Chaos Lance: *This Chaos Lord seeks to finish his foes with the first strike of his charge.*

Add 1 to the Damage characteristic and improve the Rend characteristic of this model's Chaos Lance by 2 if this model made a charge move in the same turn.

Daemonbound: *Weapons that contain the essence of a daemon are capable of swiftly devouring an enemy's soul.*

If the unmodified hit roll for an attack made with a Daemon Blade is 6, that attack inflicts 1 mortal wound on the target in addition to any normal damage.

Daggerfist: *This bladed gauntlet allows the wielder to swiftly counter enemy blows at close quarters.*

If the unmodified save roll for an attack made with a melee weapon that targets a model with a Daggerfist is 6, the attacking unit suffers 1 mortal wound after all of its attacks have been resolved.

Territorial Predator: *Any who stray into the territory of a Manticore are as good as dead, especially larger creatures that can be seen as a potential rival.*

You can re-roll hit rolls for attacks made with this model's Honed Fangs and Claws if the target is a MONSTER.

COMMAND ABILITIES

Iron-willed Overlord: *Manticores are berserk killers, and any Chaos Lord who rides one to battle displays such obvious dominance that none would dare deny his orders.*

You can use this command ability in your hero phase. If you do so, pick 1 friendly CHAOS WARRIORS unit wholly within 18" of a friendly model with this command ability. You can re-roll charge rolls and battleshock tests for that unit until your next hero phase.

KEYWORDS	CHAOS, MORTAL, MANTICORE, SLAVES TO DARKNESS, MARK OF CHAOS, EYE OF THE GODS, MONSTER, HERO, CHAOS LORD

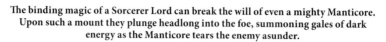

CHAOS SORCERER LORD
ON MANTICORE

MOVE ☀ **SAVE** 4+
WOUNDS 12
BRAVERY 8

The binding magic of a Sorcerer Lord can break the will of even a mighty Manticore. Upon such a mount they plunge headlong into the foe, summoning gales of dark energy as the Manticore tears the enemy asunder.

MELEE WEAPONS	Range	Attacks	To Hit	To Wound	Rend	Damage
Sorcerous Reaping Staff	2"	3	3+	3+	-1	D3
Honed Fangs and Claws	1"	5	3+	☀	-1	2
Shredding Tail	3"	☀	4+	4+	-	1

DAMAGE TABLE			
Wounds Suffered	Move	Honed Fangs and Claws	Shredding Tail
0-2	12"	1+	5
3-4	10"	2+	4
5-7	8"	3+	3
8-9	6"	4+	2
10+	6"	5+	1

DESCRIPTION

A Chaos Sorcerer Lord on Manticore is a single model armed with a Sorcerous Reaping Staff.

FLY: This model can fly.

MOUNT: This model's Manticore attacks with its Honed Fangs and Claws and Shredding Tail.

MARK OF CHAOS: When you select this model to be part of your army, you must give it one of the following Mark of Chaos keywords: **TZEENTCH**, **NURGLE**, **SLAANESH** or **UNDIVIDED**.

ABILITIES

Oracular Visions: *A sorcerer can temporarily bestow the gift of foresight upon their allies, helping them ward against oncoming enemy blows.*

In your hero phase, you can pick 1 friendly **MORTAL SLAVES TO DARKNESS** unit wholly within 12" of this model. If you do so, you can re-roll save rolls for attacks that target that unit until your next hero phase.

Territorial Predator: *Any who stray into the territory of a Manticore are as good as dead, especially larger creatures that can be seen as a potential rival.*

You can re-roll hit rolls for attacks made with this model's Honed Fangs and Claws if the target is a **MONSTER**.

MAGIC

This model is a **WIZARD**. It can attempt to cast 1 spell in your hero phase and attempt to unbind 1 spell in the enemy hero phase. It knows the Arcane Bolt, Mystic Shield and Wind of Chaos spells.

Wind of Chaos: *The sorcerer summons the raw power of Chaos and sends a vortex of fell energies screaming across the battlefield.*

Winds of Chaos has a casting value of 7. If successfully cast, pick 1 enemy unit within 18" of the caster and visible to them. Roll a number of dice equal to the number of models in that unit. For each 5, that unit suffers 1 mortal wound. For each 6, that unit suffers D3 mortal wounds.

KEYWORDS	CHAOS, MORTAL, MANTICORE, SLAVES TO DARKNESS, MARK OF CHAOS, EYE OF THE GODS, MONSTER, HERO, WIZARD, CHAOS SORCERER LORD

CHAOS LORD
ON DAEMONIC MOUNT

MOVE 10"
WOUNDS 8
SAVE 4+
BRAVERY 8

Particularly favoured Chaos Lords may be granted a daemonic steed to bear them into battle. These champions become the rulers of feared cavalry warbands, driving their mounted brethren into battle with roared oaths to the Dark Gods.

MELEE WEAPONS	Range	Attacks	To Hit	To Wound	Rend	Damage
Cursed Warhammer	1"	4	3+	3+	-1	2
Mighty Hooves	1"	3	4+	3+	-	1

DESCRIPTION

A Chaos Lord on Daemonic Mount is a single model armed with a Cursed Warhammer and Chaos Runeshield.

MOUNT: This model's Daemonic Mount attacks with its Mighty Hooves.

MARK OF CHAOS: When you select this model to be part of your army, you must give it one of the following Mark of Chaos keywords: **KHORNE**, **TZEENTCH**, **NURGLE**, **SLAANESH** or **UNDIVIDED**.

ABILITIES

Chaos Runeshield: *The dark runes inscribed upon these shields grant them the power to withstand even the most powerful attacks.*

Roll a dice each time you allocate a mortal wound to this model. On a 5+, that mortal wound is negated.

Cursed Warhammer: *Those struck by this malevolent weapon are soon blasted apart in an explosion of unholy power.*

If the unmodified hit roll for an attack made with a Cursed Warhammer is 6, that attack inflicts 2 mortal wounds on the target and the attack sequence ends (do not make a wound or save roll).

Fuelled by Carnage: *Those Chaos Lords who rise high in the favour of the gods find themselves sustained by the act of killing alone.*

At the end of the combat phase, if any enemy models were slain by wounds inflicted by this model's Cursed Warhammer in that phase, you can heal up to D3 wounds allocated to this model.

COMMAND ABILITIES

The Knights of Chaos: *This Chaos Lord commands his mounted brethren to seek and destroy the foe with renewed hatred.*

You can use this command ability in your hero phase. If you do so, pick 1 friendly **CHAOS KNIGHTS**, **CHAOS CHARIOTS** or **GOREBEAST CHARIOTS** unit wholly within 18" of a friendly **SLAVES TO DARKNESS HERO** with this command ability. You can re-roll charge rolls for that unit and add 1 to hit rolls for attacks made by that unit until your next hero phase. The same unit cannot benefit from this command ability more than once per turn.

KEYWORDS | CHAOS, DAEMON, MORTAL, SLAVES TO DARKNESS, MARK OF CHAOS, EYE OF THE GODS, HERO, CHAOS LORD

MOVE **9"**

WOUNDS **9**

SAVE **3+**

8

BRAVERY

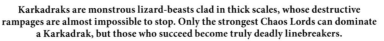

CHAOS LORD
ON KARKADRAK

Karkadraks are monstrous lizard-beasts clad in thick scales, whose destructive rampages are almost impossible to stop. Only the strongest Chaos Lords can dominate a Karkadrak, but those who succeed become truly deadly linebreakers.

MELEE WEAPONS	Range	Attacks	To Hit	To Wound	Rend	Damage
Hexed Battle-axe	1"	5	3+	3+	-	2
Daemonbound Blade	1"	3	3+	3+	-1	D3
Tearing Horn and Claws	1"	3	4+	3+	-1	2
Battering Tail	1"	2	4+	4+	-	1

DESCRIPTION

A Chaos Lord on Karkadrak is a single model armed with a Hexed Battle-axe and Daemonbound Blade.

MOUNT: This model's Karkadrak attacks with its Tearing Horn and Claws and its Battering Tail.

MARK OF CHAOS: When you select this model to be part of your army, you must give it one of the following Mark of Chaos keywords: **Khorne**, **Tzeentch**, **Nurgle**, **Slaanesh** or **Undivided**.

ABILITIES

Brutish Rampage: *A charging Karkadrak is an almost unstoppable force, capable of smashing straight through even the most determined shieldwall.*

Roll a dice for each enemy unit that is within 1" of this model after this model makes a charge move. On a 2+, that unit suffers D3 mortal wounds.

Daemonbound: *Weapons that contain the essence of a daemon are capable of swiftly devouring an enemy's soul.*

If the unmodified hit roll for an attack made with a Daemonbound Blade is 6, that attack inflicts 1 mortal wound on the target in addition to any normal damage.

Fuelled by Carnage: *Those Chaos Lords who rise high in the favour of the gods find themselves sustained by the act of killing alone.*

At the end of the combat phase, if any enemy models were slain by wounds inflicted by this model's Hexed Battle-axe in that phase, you can heal up to D3 wounds allocated to this model.

Rune-etched Plating: *The symbols carved across the armour of this champion radiate an aura of fell power that protects the wearer from harm.*

Roll a dice each time you allocate a mortal wound to this model. On a 5+, that mortal wound is negated.

COMMAND ABILITIES

The Knights of Chaos: *This Chaos Lord commands his mounted brethren to seek and destroy the foe with renewed hatred.*

You can use this command ability in your hero phase. If you do so, pick 1 friendly **Chaos Knights**, **Chaos Chariots** or **Gorebeast Chariots** unit wholly within 18" of a friendly **Slaves to Darkness Hero** with this command ability. Until your next hero phase, you can re-roll charge rolls for that unit and add 1 to hit rolls for attacks made by that unit. The same unit cannot benefit from this command ability more than once per turn.

KEYWORDS	CHAOS, MORTAL, SLAVES TO DARKNESS, MARK OF CHAOS, EYE OF THE GODS, HERO, CHAOS LORD

CHAOS LORD

95

Chaos Lords are dark champions who have walked the Path to Glory and are now only one step away from glory or damnation. They are the rulers of great warbands and hordes, and their followers will die before failing these fearsome warlords.

MELEE WEAPONS	Range	Attacks	To Hit	To Wound	Rend	Damage
Reaperblade	2"	3	3+	3+	-2	2
Daemonbound Steel	1"	3	3+	3+	-1	1
Daemonbound War-flail	2"	6	4+	4+	-2	1

DESCRIPTION

A Chaos Lord is a single model armed with one of the following weapon options: Reaperblade and Daemonbound Steel; or Daemonbound War-flail.

MARK OF CHAOS: When you select this model to be part of your army, you must give it one of the following Mark of Chaos keywords: KHORNE, TZEENTCH, NURGLE, SLAANESH or UNDIVIDED.

ABILITIES

Daemonbound: *Weapons that contain the essence of a daemon are capable of swiftly devouring an enemy's soul.*

If the unmodified hit roll for an attack made with a Daemonbound weapon is 6, that attack inflicts 1 mortal wound on the target in addition to any normal damage.

COMMAND ABILITIES

Spurred by the Gods: *Chaos Lords are the favoured of the dark pantheon, and in their*

presence their warriors fight all the harder.

You can use this command ability at the start of the combat phase. If you do so, pick 1 friendly MORTAL SLAVES TO DARKNESS unit wholly within 12" of a friendly model with this command ability. After that unit has fought in that phase for the first time, when it is your turn to pick a unit to fight with later in the same phase, that unit can be selected to fight for a second time if it is within 3" of any enemy units. The same unit cannot benefit from this command ability more than once per turn.

KEYWORDS	CHAOS, MORTAL, SLAVES TO DARKNESS, MARK OF CHAOS, EYE OF THE GODS, HERO, CHAOS LORD

CHAOS SORCERER LORD

The very air around a Sorcerer Lord is saturated with dark magic. With their command of daemonic powers and gift of foresight, these warlocks bolster the power of their allies while unleashing their own devastating spellcraft on the enemy.

MELEE WEAPONS	Range	Attacks	To Hit	To Wound	Rend	Damage
Sorcerer Staff	2"	1	4+	3+	-1	D3
Chaos Runeblade	1"	2	3+	3+	-	1

DESCRIPTION

A Chaos Sorcerer Lord is a single model armed with a Sorcerer Staff and Chaos Runeblade.

MARK OF CHAOS: When you select this model to be part of your army, you must give it one of the following Mark of Chaos keywords: NURGLE, TZEENTCH, SLAANESH or UNDIVIDED.

ABILITIES

Oracular Visions: *A sorcerer can temporarily bestow the gift of foresight upon their allies, helping them ward against oncoming enemy blows.*

In your hero phase, you can pick 1 friendly MORTAL SLAVES TO DARKNESS unit wholly within 12" of this model. If you do so, you can re-roll save rolls for attacks that target that unit until your next hero phase.

MAGIC

This model is a WIZARD. It can attempt to cast 1 spell in your hero phase and attempt to unbind 1 spell in the enemy hero phase. It knows the Arcane Bolt, Mystic Shield and Daemonic Power spells.

Daemonic Power: *The sorcerer bestows his followers with daemonic essence, boosting their skill and strength to unholy levels.*

Daemonic Power has a casting value of 6. If successfully cast, pick 1 friendly MORTAL SLAVES TO DARKNESS unit wholly within 18" of the caster and visible to them. You can re-roll hit and wound rolls for attacks made by that unit until your next hero phase.

KEYWORDS	CHAOS, MORTAL, SLAVES TO DARKNESS, MARK OF CHAOS, EYE OF THE GODS, HERO, WIZARD, CHAOS SORCERER LORD

● WARSCROLL ●

EXALTED HERO OF CHAOS

MOVE	5"
WOUNDS	5
SAVE	4+
BRAVERY	8

Exalted Heroes are those warriors who have caught the notice of the gods and now seek to make a true name for themselves. Their favoured prey are monsters and enemy champions, for by slaying these foes an Exalted Hero proves their own might.

MELEE WEAPONS	Range	Attacks	To Hit	To Wound	Rend	Damage
Rune-etched Blades	1"	D6	3+	3+	-1	1

DESCRIPTION

An Exalted Hero of Chaos is a single model armed with Rune-etched Blades.

MARK OF CHAOS: When you select this model to be part of your army, you must give it one of the following Mark of Chaos keywords: **KHORNE, TZEENTCH, NURGLE, SLAANESH** or **UNDIVIDED.**

ABILITIES

Dark Blessings: *Exalted Heroes of Chaos are watched with interest by the gods, who will sometimes intervene to protect the latest objects of their fickle curiosity.*

Roll a dice each time you allocate a mortal wound to this model. On a 5+, that mortal wound is negated.

Glory-hungry Bladesman: *Exalted Heroes scour the battlefield for worthy foes to slay in the name of the Dark Gods.*

Add 1 to hit rolls for attacks made by this model if the target is a **HERO** or **MONSTER.**

Thrice-damned Dagger: *Exalted Heroes carve out the hearts of powerful enemies they have slain, devouring the organ to inherit their might.*

If this model makes an attack with a melee weapon that slays one or more enemy **HEROES**

or **MONSTERS,** you can heal up to D3 wounds allocated to this model after all of its attacks have been resolved.

Trail of Red Ruin: *This warrior's bloodlust can never be satisfied, constantly pushing him forward in search of new challenges.*

If this model made a charge move this turn, after this model has fought in the combat phase for the first time, it can immediately fight for a second time if it is within 3" of an enemy unit.

KEYWORDS	CHAOS, MORTAL, SLAVES TO DARKNESS, MARK OF CHAOS, EYE OF THE GODS, HERO, EXALTED HERO OF CHAOS

● WARSCROLL ●

OGROID MYRMIDON

MOVE	6"
WOUNDS	8
SAVE	4+
BRAVERY	8

Myrmidons are masters of the Varanspire's fighting pits, and have spent decades mastering the gladiatorial arts. In battle they lead those who seek to join the Everchosen's legions, for to impress a Myrmidon is to be marked for glory.

MISSILE WEAPONS	Range	Attacks	To Hit	To Wound	Rend	Damage
Gladiator Spear	18"	1	3+	3+	-1	D3
MELEE WEAPONS	**Range**	**Attacks**	**To Hit**	**To Wound**	**Rend**	**Damage**
Gladiator Spear	2"	6	3+	3+	-1	1
Great Horns	1"	1	3+	3+	-2	3

DESCRIPTION

An Ogroid Myrmidon is a single model armed with a Gladiator Spear and Great Horns.

ABILITIES

Arcane Fury: *The magical runes carved into a Myrmidon's flesh glow with a blood-red light, their energies empowering the Ogroid's blows.*

If the unmodified hit roll for an attack made with a melee weapon by this model is 6, that attack

scores 2 hits on the target instead of 1. Make a wound and save roll for each hit.

Berserk Rage: *Every wound inflicted on a Myrmidon only serves to stoke its rage further.*

You can re-roll hit and wound rolls for attacks made with melee weapons by this model if any wounds or mortal wounds were allocated to this model earlier in the same phase.

COMMAND ABILITIES

Pit Marshal: *Myrmidons rule the gladiatorial arenas of the Eightpoints, and those pit fighter warbands they lead into battle are spurred to greater acts of carnage by their presence.*

You can use this command ability in the combat phase. If you do so, pick 1 friendly **CULTISTS** unit wholly within 12" of a friendly model with this command ability. Do not take battleshock tests for that unit until the start of your next hero phase.

KEYWORDS	CHAOS, MORTAL, SLAVES TO DARKNESS, HERO, EYE OF THE GODS, OGROID MYRMIDON

BE'LAKOR

97

Be'lakor is unique amongst his ascended kin, the only Daemon Prince ever to be blessed by all four of the Brothers in Darkness. A creature of shadow and deception, those caught in his manipulations do not realise their doom until it is too late.

MELEE WEAPONS	Range	Attacks	To Hit	To Wound	Rend	Damage
Blade of Shadows	1"	6	3+	3+	-1	2

MOVE 12"
WOUNDS 8
SAVE 4+
BRAVERY 10

DESCRIPTION

Be'lakor is a named character that is a single model. He is armed with the Blade of Shadows.

FLY: This model can fly.

ABILITIES

The Dark Master: *Many puppets dance on Be'lakor's infernal strings, though few realise as much until their fate is sealed.*

After set-up is complete but before the first battle round begins, secretly pick 1 enemy unit on the battlefield. Once per battle, at the start of the enemy hero phase, you can reveal which unit you picked.

Until your next hero phase, your opponent must roll a dice each time that unit attempts to cast a spell, move, charge or attack with any weapons it is armed with. On a 1-4, that unit cannot do so. On a 5+, that unit can do so as normal.

Lord of Torment: *Be'lakor is invigorated by the suffering and terror of mortals.*

If an enemy unit fails a battleshock test while it is within 10" of this model, you can heal up to D3 wounds allocated to this model.

Shadow Form: *Be'lakor's physical form is as insubstantial as the cloying mists of Ulgu, and just as hard to land a telling blow against.*

Ignore modifiers (positive or negative) when making save rolls for attacks that target this model.

MAGIC

Be'lakor is a **WIZARD**. He can attempt to cast 2 spells in your hero phase and attempt to unbind 2 spells in the enemy hero phase. He knows the Arcane Bolt, Mystic Shield and Enfeeble Foe spells.

Enfeeble Foe: *With a series of hissed incantations, Be'lakor instils visions of loss and despair in the minds of his enemies to drain them of their fighting spirit.*

Enfeeble Foe has a casting value of 6. If successfully cast, pick 1 enemy unit within 18" of the caster and visible to them. Subtract 1 from wound rolls for attacks made with melee weapons by that unit until your next hero phase.

KEYWORDS	CHAOS, DAEMON, SLAVES TO DARKNESS, UNDIVIDED, HERO, WIZARD, DAEMON PRINCE, BE'LAKOR

SLAVES TO DARKNESS
DAEMON PRINCE

MOVE 12"
SAVE 3+
WOUNDS 8
BRAVERY 10

98

Those champions who consistently please their patron god may eventually be granted immortality as a Daemon Prince. Each of these black-hearted monsters is a living icon of their master's power, and a terrifying foe to face on the battlefield.

MELEE WEAPONS	Range	Attacks	To Hit	To Wound	Rend	Damage
Daemonic Axe	1"	3	3+	3+	-2	2
Hellforged Sword	2"	4	4+	3+	-1	D3
Malefic Talons	1"	3	3+	3+	-	2

DESCRIPTION

A Slaves to Darkness Daemon Prince is a single model armed with one of the following weapon options: Daemonic Axe and Malefic Talons; or Hellforged Sword and Malefic Talons.

FLY: This model can fly.

MARK OF CHAOS: When you select this model to be part of your army, you must give it one of the following Mark of Chaos keywords: **KHORNE**, **TZEENTCH**, **NURGLE** or **SLAANESH**.

ABILITIES

Bounding Charge: *Little can hope to stand before the fury of a charging Daemon Prince.*

Add 1 to hit rolls for attacks made by this model if it charged in the same turn.

Hellforged Sword: *This sword can carve through armour and flesh as if they were made of nothing more than paper.*

If the unmodified hit roll for an attack made with a Hellforged Sword is 6, that attack inflicts 2 mortal wounds on the target and the attack sequence ends (do not make a wound or save roll).

Immortal Champion: *Those favoured enough to ascend to daemonhood are among the most deadly servants of the Ruinous Powers.*

This model fights at the start of the combat phase. This model cannot fight again in that phase unless an ability or spell allows it to fight more than once.

COMMAND ABILITIES

Bloodslick Ground: *The Daemon Prince summons pools of thick gore around itself to hinder the movement of its enemies.*

You can use this command ability in your hero phase if this model has the **KHORNE** keyword. If you do so, until your next hero phase, run and charge rolls made for enemy units within 18" of this model are halved. You cannot use this command ability more than once per turn.

Arcane Influence: *The Daemon Prince harnesses a fraction of Tzeentch's arcane might.*

You can use this command ability at the start of your hero phase if this model has the **TZEENTCH** keyword. If you do so, pick 1 friendly **SLAVES TO DARKNESS WIZARD** wholly within 12" of this model. Add 1 to casting rolls for that unit until the end of that phase.

Bloated Blessings: *The Daemon Prince gifts their followers with pestilent pustules that spray bile and corrosive acid when burst open.*

You can use this command ability at the start of your hero phase if this model has the **NURGLE** keyword. If you do so, pick 1 friendly **SLAVES TO DARKNESS NURGLE** unit wholly within 12" of this model. Until your next hero phase, if the unmodified hit roll for an attack that targets that unit is 6, the attacking unit suffers D3 mortal wounds after all of its attacks have been resolved.

Revel in Agony: *The deadly mania of this Daemon Prince and their followers only grows as they suffer blissful injury.*

You can use this command ability at the start of the combat phase if this model has the **SLAANESH** keyword. If you do so, until your next hero phase, if any models from a friendly **SLAVES TO DARKNESS SLAANESH** unit wholly within 12" of this model are slain by an attack made with a melee weapon by an enemy unit, add 1 to hit rolls for attacks made by that friendly unit that target that enemy unit until your next hero phase. You cannot use this command ability more than once per turn.

KEYWORDS	CHAOS, DAEMON, SLAVES TO DARKNESS, HERO, MARK OF CHAOS, DAEMON PRINCE

DARKOATH WARQUEEN

MOVE	6"
WOUNDS	6
SAVE	5+
	8
BRAVERY	

99

A Darkoath Warqueen has proven herself the rightful ruler of her barbarian tribesfolk time and again. She has sworn dread pacts to bring carnage to the Mortal Realms, and all who stand in her way must face both her wrath and that of her devoted warriors.

MELEE WEAPONS	Range	Attacks	To Hit	To Wound	Rend	Damage
Rune-etched Axe	1"	6	3+	3+	-1	1

DESCRIPTION

A Darkoath Warqueen is a single model. She is armed with a Rune-etched Axe and carries an Infernal Runeshield.

ABILITIES

Infernal Runeshield: *Inscribed with the runes of the barbarian tribes she has conquered, the Darkoath Warqueen's shield is blessed with daemonic power.*

Roll a dice each time you allocate a wound or mortal wound to this model. On a 6, that wound or mortal wound is negated and the attacking unit suffers 1 mortal wound.

Savage Duellist: *A Darkoath Warqueen is empowered by acts of personal conquest; when she fixes her gaze on a powerful foe in single combat, her battle-frenzy reaches new heights.*

This model fights at the start of the combat phase. This model cannot fight again in that phase unless an ability or spell allows it to fight more than once.

In addition, add 1 to the Damage characteristic of this model's Rune-etched Axe if the target is a **Hero** or **Monster**.

COMMAND ABILITIES

The Will of the Gods: *A Darkoath Warqueen speaks with irresistible authority, for she has heard the wishes of the Chaos Gods. When she calls for her tribespeople to begin the slaughter, they are spurred to an all-out charge.*

You can use this command ability at the start of your charge phase. If you do so, until the end of that phase, add 3 to charge rolls for friendly **Chaos Marauders** and **Cultists** units wholly within 12" this model when the charge roll is made. A unit cannot benefit from this command ability more than once per phase.

KEYWORDS	CHAOS, MORTAL, SLAVES TO DARKNESS, EYE OF THE GODS, HERO, DARKOATH WARQUEEN

DARKOATH CHIEFTAIN

MOVE	6"
WOUNDS	6
SAVE	5+
	8
BRAVERY	

Darkoath Chieftains lead their barbarian tribes to war with the fury and conviction of the truly devoted. These masterful warriors are always seeking greater challenges, and their skill-at-arms is spoken of in awe by their followers.

MELEE WEAPONS	Range	Attacks	To Hit	To Wound	Rend	Damage
Warlord Axe	1"	1	3+	3+	-	1
Cursed Broadsword	1"	3	4+	3+	-1	2

DESCRIPTION

A Darkoath Chieftain is a single model, armed with a Warlord Axe and Cursed Broadsword.

ABILITIES

Berserk Charge: *A Darkoath Chieftain is on a constant quest for glory, charging into every battle with boundless ferocity.*

Add 3 to the Attacks characteristic of this model's Cursed Broadsword if it charged in the same turn.

Deathblow: *Darkoath Chieftains are superlative warriors, and once the slaughter has begun their furious blows inevitably reap a fearsome toll of lives.*

At the end of the combat phase, if any enemy models were slain by this model in that phase, each enemy unit within 1" of this model suffers 1 mortal wound.

COMMAND ABILITIES

Last Gasp of Glory: *The Darkoath Chieftain exhorts the barbarian tribes they rule to fight on even as death claims them.*

You can use this command ability at the start of the combat phase. If you do so, pick a friendly model with this command ability. Until the end of the phase, friendly **Chaos Marauders** and **Cultists** models that are slain within 12" of the model you picked and have not yet fought in that phase can fight before being removed from play.

KEYWORDS	CHAOS, MORTAL, SLAVES TO DARKNESS, HERO, EYE OF THE GODS, DARKOATH CHIEFTAIN

THEDDRA SKULL-SCRYER

MOVE	6"
WOUNDS	5
SAVE	5+
BRAVERY	7

100

Guided by searing visions of conquest and glory, the God-speaker known as Theddra Skull-Scryer leads warriors from the Tribe of the Black Fang through a combination of ruthlessness and awesome displays of gods-given power.

MELEE WEAPONS	Range	Attacks	To Hit	To Wound	Rend	Damage
Darkoath Wand	1"	2	4+	3+	-1	D3

DESCRIPTION

Theddra Skull-Scryer is a named character that is a single model. She is armed with a Darkoath Wand.

ABILITIES

Pact of Soul and Iron: *Every member of the Godsworn Hunt has sworn a blood-oath to hunt down and kill the upstart God-King's so-called Stormcast Eternals.*

You can re-roll hit rolls for attacks made by this model. In addition, you can re-roll wound rolls for attacks made by this model that target a **STORMCAST ETERNAL** unit.

MAGIC

Theddra Skull-Scryer is a **WIZARD**. She can attempt to cast 1 spell in your hero phase and attempt to unbind 1 spell in the enemy hero phase. She knows the Arcane Bolt, Mystic Shield and Enfeeblement spells.

Enfeeblement: *Waves of withering energy flood over Skull-Scryer's foes.*

Enfeeblement has a casting value of 6. If successfully cast, pick 1 enemy unit within 12" of the caster that is visible to them. Subtract 1 from wound rolls for attacks made with melee weapons by that unit until your next hero phase.

KEYWORDS	CHAOS, MORTAL, SLAVES TO DARKNESS, HERO, WIZARD, GOD-SPEAKER, THEDDRA SKULL-SCRYER

GODSWORN HUNT

MOVE	6"
WOUNDS	1
SAVE	6+
BRAVERY	6

The Godsworn Hunt is formed of the greatest champions of the Tribe of the Black Fang. Each is a hardened killer who has earned their name through bloody deeds, and their bodies are bedecked with gruesome trophies and oath-stones.

MISSILE WEAPONS	Range	Attacks	To Hit	To Wound	Rend	Damage
Hunting Bow	24"	2	4+	4+	-	1
Ensorcelled Javelin	12"	1	3+	3+	-1	D3
MELEE WEAPONS	Range	Attacks	To Hit	To Wound	Rend	Damage
Darkoath Knife	1"	3	4+	4+	-	1
Great Weapon	1"	2	4+	3+	-1	2
Hunting Bow	1"	1	4+	5+	-	1
Savage Bite	1"	2	3+	3+	-	1

DESCRIPTION

The Godsworn Hunt is a unit that has 5 models. Jagathra is armed with an Ensorcelled Javelin and Darkoath Knife; Shond Head-Claimer and Grundann Blood-Eye are each armed with a Great Weapon; Ollo is armed with a Hunting Bow; and Grawl is armed with a Savage Bite.

ABILITIES

Pact of Soul and Iron: *Every member of the Godsworn Hunt has sworn a blood-oath to hunt down and kill the upstart God-King's so-called Stormcast Eternals.*

You can re-roll hit rolls for attacks made by this unit. In addition, you can re-roll wound rolls for attacks made by this unit that target a **STORMCAST ETERNAL** unit.

KEYWORDS	CHAOS, MORTAL, SLAVES TO DARKNESS, GODSWORN HUNT

CHAOS WARSHRINE

Carried to battle by two huge mutants, Chaos Warshrines are tributes to the glory of the dark pantheon. From atop the raised platform a Shrine Keeper beseeches the gods for their boon, granting their blessings to the legions of darkness.

MELEE WEAPONS	Range	Attacks	To Hit	To Wound	Rend	Damage
Sacrificial Blade	1"	4	3+	3+	-1	2
Flailing Fists	1"	✸	4+	3+	-	2

DAMAGE TABLE			
Wounds Suffered	Move	Flailing Fists	Protection of the Dark Gods
0-2	8"	6	18"
3-4	7"	5	12"
5-7	6"	4	9"
8-9	5"	3	6"
10+	4"	2	3"

DESCRIPTION

A Chaos Warshrine is a single model armed with a Sacrificial Blade.

MOUNT: This model's Shrine Bearers attack with their Flailing Fists.

MARK OF CHAOS: When you select this model to be part of your army, you must give it one of the following Mark of Chaos keywords: **KHORNE**, **TZEENTCH**, **NURGLE**, **SLAANESH** or **UNDIVIDED**.

ABILITIES

Protection of the Dark Gods: *Worshippers of the Ruinous Powers gather around these shrines in the hope of receiving divine protection.*

Roll a dice each time you allocate a wound or mortal wound to a friendly **MORTAL SLAVES TO DARKNESS** unit wholly within the range of the Protection of the Dark Gods ability for this model shown on the damage table above. On a 6, that wound or mortal wound is negated.

Favour of the Ruinous Powers: *A Shrinemaster invokes the dark pantheon to bless nearby followers with their favour.*

At the start your hero phase, you can say that this model will chant one of the following prayers. If you do so, pick 1 friendly **MORTAL SLAVES TO DARKNESS** unit wholly within 18" of this model and make a prayer roll by rolling a dice. On a 1-2, the prayer is not answered. On a 3+, the prayer is answered. The same unit cannot benefit from the same prayer more than once per turn.

Favour of Khorne: You can re-roll charge rolls for that unit until your next hero phase.

In addition, if that unit has the **KHORNE** keyword, you can re-roll hit rolls for attacks made with melee weapons by that unit until your next hero phase.

Favour of Tzeentch: You can re-roll save rolls for attacks that target that unit until your next hero phase.

In addition, if that unit has the **TZEENTCH** keyword, until your next hero phase, each time that unit is affected by a spell or endless spell, you can roll a dice. If you do so, on a 4+, ignore the effects of that spell or endless spell on that unit.

Favour of Nurgle: You can re-roll wound rolls for attacks made with melee weapons by that unit until your next hero phase.

In addition, if that unit has the **NURGLE** keyword, add 1 to save rolls for attacks that target that unit until your next hero phase.

Favour of Slaanesh: You can re-roll charge rolls for that unit until your next hero phase.

In addition, if that unit has the **SLAANESH** keyword, do not take battleshock tests for that unit until your next hero phase.

Favour of Chaos: You can re-roll hit and wound rolls for attacks made by that unit until your next hero phase.

In addition, if that unit has the **UNDIVIDED** keyword, you can re-roll charge rolls for that unit until your next hero phase.

KEYWORDS	CHAOS, MORTAL, SLAVES TO DARKNESS, TOTEM, PRIEST, MARK OF CHAOS, CHAOS WARSHRINE

MOVE	6"
WOUNDS	2
SAVE	4+
BRAVERY	7

CHAOS CHOSEN

Devotees of Chaos who garner many dark rewards may rise to the ranks of the Chosen. Armed with wicked soul-cleaving blades, these champions fight at the forefront of the Chaotic hordes, inspiring their brethren through acts of brutal violence.

MELEE WEAPONS	Range	Attacks	To Hit	To Wound	Rend	Damage
Soul Splitter	1"	3	3+	3+	-1	1

DESCRIPTION

A unit of Chaos Chosen has any number of models, each armed with a Soul Splitter.

EXALTED CHAMPION: 1 model in this unit can be an Exalted Champion. Add 1 to the Attacks characteristic of that model's melee weapon.

ICON BEARER: 1 in every 5 models in this unit can be an Icon Bearer. Subtract 1 from the Bravery characteristic of enemy units while they are within 6" of any friendly Icon Bearers.

SKULL DRUMMER: 1 in every 5 models in this unit can be a Skull Drummer. Add 1 to run and charge rolls for this unit while it includes any Skull Drummers.

MARK OF CHAOS: When you select this unit to be part of your army, you must give it one of the following Mark of Chaos keywords: KHORNE, TZEENTCH, NURGLE, SLAANESH or UNDIVIDED.

ABILITIES

Slaughter-leaders: *The Chosen inspire their kin through acts of excessive bloodshed and violence.*

If a model from this unit makes an attack that slays one or more enemy models, after all of this unit's attacks have been resolved, you can re-roll wound rolls for attacks made by friendly MORTAL SLAVES TO DARKNESS units wholly within 12" of any friendly unit with this ability until your next hero phase.

Soul Splitter: *One blow from a Soul Splitter can cleave even a fully armoured warrior in twain.*

If the unmodified hit roll for an attack made with a Soul Splitter is 6, that attack inflicts 1 mortal wound on the target in addition to any normal damage.

KEYWORDS	CHAOS, MORTAL, SLAVES TO DARKNESS, MARK OF CHAOS, CHAOS CHOSEN

MOVE	2D6"
WOUNDS	5
SAVE	5+
BRAVERY	10

SLAVES TO DARKNESS
CHAOS SPAWN

Those who receive too many gifts from the gods may degenerate into a hideous Chaos Spawn. Lumpen and misformed, these creatures lurch from their lairs when death is on the wind, slaughtering all before them with flailing tentacles and crooked claws.

MELEE WEAPONS	Range	Attacks	To Hit	To Wound	Rend	Damage
Freakish Mutations	1"	2D6	4+	4+	-	1

DESCRIPTION

A unit of Slaves to Darkness Chaos Spawn has any number of models, each armed with Freakish Mutations.

MARK OF CHAOS: When you select this unit to be part of your army, you must give it one of the following Mark of Chaos keywords: KHORNE, TZEENTCH, NURGLE, SLAANESH or UNDIVIDED.

ABILITIES

Writhing Tentacles: *The body of a Chaos Spawn is ever in flux, making them wildly unpredictable adversaries.*

If you roll a double when determining the number of attacks made by Freakish Mutations, add 1 to hit and wound rolls for attacks made by the attacking model until the end of the phase.

KEYWORDS	CHAOS, MORTAL, SLAVES TO DARKNESS, MARK OF CHAOS, CHAOS SPAWN

CHAOS CHARIOTS

MOVE 12"
WOUNDS 7
SAVE 4+
BRAVERY 6

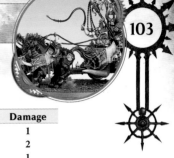

Swift Chaos Chariots thunder across the plains hunting for fresh prey. Drawn by corrupted steeds, the momentum of these constructs is a weapon of its own, and the charioteers take dark pleasure in crushing enemies beneath their heavy wheels.

MELEE WEAPONS	Range	Attacks	To Hit	To Wound	Rend	Damage
Lashing Whip	2"	2	4+	4+	-	1
Chaos Greatblade	2"	2	3+	3+	-1	2
Chaos War-flail	2"	D6	4+	3+	-	1
Trampling Hooves	1"	4	4+	4+	-	1

DESCRIPTION

A unit of Chaos Chariots has any number of models, each armed with one of the following weapon options: Chaos Greatblade and Lashing Whip; or Chaos War-flail and Lashing Whip.

MOUNT: This unit's War Steeds attack with their Trampling Hooves.

EXALTED CHARIOTEER: 1 model in this unit can be an Exalted Charioteer. Add 1 to hit rolls for attacks made with melee weapons by that model (excluding those of its mount).

MARK OF CHAOS: When you select this unit to be part of your army, you must give it one of the following Mark of Chaos keywords: **KHORNE**, **TZEENTCH**, **NURGLE**, **SLAANESH** or **UNDIVIDED**.

ABILITIES

Don't Spare the Lash: *These cruel charioteers know how to get the most out of their beasts of burden.*

Once per battle, this unit can run and still charge later in the same turn.

Swift Death: *Chaos Chariots are at their most deadly on the charge, where their considerable bulk and bladed wheels can cause untold devastation.*

After this unit makes a charge move, you can pick 1 enemy unit within 1" of this unit and roll a number of dice equal to the charge roll for that charge move. For each 5+, that enemy unit suffers 1 mortal wound.

KEYWORDS | CHAOS, MORTAL, SLAVES TO DARKNESS, MARK OF CHAOS, CHAOS CHARIOTS

GOREBEAST CHARIOTS

MOVE 9"
WOUNDS 8
SAVE 4+
BRAVERY 6

Those chariots pulled by hulking Gorebeasts are gloriously brutal weapons. Only the strongest of will can break a Gorebeast, and when in the thick of combat these creatures rip their foes limb from limb with shocking ferocity.

MELEE WEAPONS	Range	Attacks	To Hit	To Wound	Rend	Damage
Lashing Whip	2"	2	4+	4+	-	1
Chaos Greatblade	2"	2	3+	3+	-1	2
Chaos War-flail	2"	D6	4+	3+	-	1
Crushing Fists	1"	3	3+	3+	-	2

DESCRIPTION

A unit of Gorebeast Chariots has any number of models, each armed with one of the following weapon options: Chaos Greatblade and Lashing Whip; or Chaos War-flail and Lashing Whip.

MOUNT: This unit's Gorebeasts attack with their Crushing Fists.

EXALTED CHARIOTEER: 1 model in this unit can be an Exalted Charioteer. Add 1 to hit rolls for attacks made with melee weapons by that model (excluding those of its mount).

MARK OF CHAOS: When you select this unit to be part of your army, you must give it one of the following Mark of Chaos keywords: **KHORNE**, **TZEENTCH**, **NURGLE**, **SLAANESH** or **UNDIVIDED**.

ABILITIES

Crashing Charge: *Gorebeast Chariots crash into the enemy as a raging stampede of destruction.*

After this unit makes a charge move, roll a dice for each enemy unit within 1" of this unit. On a 2+, that enemy unit suffers D3 mortal wounds.

Explosive Brutality: *There is little as terrifying or as destructive as the sudden bursts of rage that characterise Gorebeasts.*

If you make a charge move with this unit and the unmodified charge roll was 8+, add 1 to hit and wound rolls for attacks made by this unit's Crushing Fists until your next hero phase.

KEYWORDS | CHAOS, MORTAL, SLAVES TO DARKNESS, MARK OF CHAOS, GOREBEAST CHARIOTS

	MOVE	
WOUNDS	10"	SAVE
3		4+
	7	
	BRAVERY	

104

CHAOS KNIGHTS

The coming of the Chaos Knights heralds the death of empires. These dreaded champions charge fearlessly into the deadliest of battles, striking down foes all around them with sundering blows from their ensorcelled weapons.

MELEE WEAPONS	Range	Attacks	To Hit	To Wound	Rend	Damage
Ensorcelled Weapon	1"	3	3+	3+	-1	1
Cursed Lance	2"	2	4+	3+	-	1
Cursed Flail	2"	D6	4+	3+	-	1
Trampling Hooves	1"	2	4+	4+	-	1

DESCRIPTION

A unit of Chaos Knights has any number of models, each armed with one of the following weapon options: Ensorcelled Weapon and Chaos Runeshield; or Cursed Lance and Chaos Runeshield.

MOUNT: This unit's War Steeds attack with their Trampling Hooves.

DOOM KNIGHT: 1 model in this unit can be a Doom Knight. Add 1 to the Attacks characteristic that model's melee weapons (excluding its mount). In addition, that model can replace its weapon option with a Cursed Flail and Chaos Runeshield.

STANDARD BEARER: 1 in every 5 models in this unit can be a Standard Bearer. Add 1 to the Bravery characteristic of this unit while it includes any Standard Bearers.

HORNBLOWER: 1 in every 5 models in this unit can be a Hornblower. Add 1 to run and charge rolls for a unit that includes any Hornblowers.

MARK OF CHAOS: When you select this unit to be part of your army, you must give it one of the following Mark of Chaos keywords: **KHORNE**, **TZEENTCH**, **NURGLE**, **SLAANESH** or **UNDIVIDED**.

ABILITIES

Chaos Runeshields: *The dark runes inscribed upon these shields grant them the power to withstand even the most powerful attacks.*

Roll a dice each time you allocate a mortal wound to a unit with Chaos Runeshields. On a 5+, that mortal wound is negated.

Impaling Charge: *A charging Chaos Knight who wields a lance is capable of spitting several enemies at once with the point of their ensorcelled polearm.*

Add 1 to the Damage characteristic and improve the Rend characteristic of this unit's Cursed Lances by 2 if it made a charge move in the same turn.

Terrifying Champions: *The brutal reputation of the Chaos Knights precedes them, and can inspire dread in even the stoutest heart.*

Subtract 1 from the Bravery characteristic of enemy units within 3" of any friendly units with this ability in the battleshock phase.

KEYWORDS   CHAOS, MORTAL, SLAVES TO DARKNESS, MARK OF CHAOS, CHAOS KNIGHTS

MOVE 5"
WOUNDS 2
SAVE 4+
BRAVERY 7

CHAOS WARRIORS

Clad in hellforged iron and swollen with dark blessings, Chaos Warriors are the bane of civilisation. Entire legions of these armoured killers march into battle in search of divine favour, each warrior the equal of several lesser mortals.

MELEE WEAPONS	Range	Attacks	To Hit	To Wound	Rend	Damage
Chaos Hand Weapon(s)	1"	2	3+	3+	-	1
Chaos Halberd	2"	2	3+	4+	-	1
Chaos Greatblade	1"	2	4+	3+	-1	1

DESCRIPTION

A unit of Chaos Warriors has any number of models, each armed with one of the following weapon options: Chaos Hand Weapon and Chaos Runeshield; Chaos Halberd and Chaos Runeshield; Chaos Greatblade; or pair of Chaos Hand Weapons.

ASPIRING CHAMPION: 1 model in this unit can be an Aspiring Champion. Add 1 to the Attacks characteristic of that model's melee weapons.

STANDARD BEARER: 1 in every 5 models in this unit can be a Standard Bearer. Add 1 to the Bravery characteristic of this unit while it includes any Standard Bearers.

HORNBLOWER: 1 in every 5 models in this unit can be a Hornblower. Add 1 to run and charge rolls for this unit while it includes any Hornblowers.

MARK OF CHAOS: When you select this unit to be part of your army, you must give it one of the following Mark of Chaos keywords: Khorne, Tzeentch, Nurgle, Slaanesh or Undivided.

ABILITIES

Chaos Runeshields: *The dark runes inscribed upon these shields grant them the power to withstand even the most powerful attacks.*

Roll a dice each time you allocate a mortal wound to a unit that carries Chaos Runeshields. On a 5+, that mortal wound is negated.

Legions of Chaos: *A great number of Chaos Warriors acting in concert can prove almost unstoppable.*

You can re-roll save rolls for attacks that target this unit while it has at least 10 models.

Pair of Chaos Hand Weapons: *Chaos Warriors who wield a blade in each hand can unleash a blistering flurry of strikes.*

You can re-roll hit rolls for attacks made with a pair of Chaos Hand Weapons.

KEYWORDS | CHAOS, MORTAL, SLAVES TO DARKNESS, MARK OF CHAOS, CHAOS WARRIORS

CHAOS MARAUDERS

MOVE 6"
SAVE 6+
BRAVERY 5
WOUNDS 1

106

Hordes of Chaos Marauders form the backbone of many Slaves to Darkness tribes. These barbarous warriors number in the thousands, and fight ferociously to sweep away civilisation in the name of the Chaos Gods.

MELEE WEAPONS	Range	Attacks	To Hit	To Wound	Rend	Damage
Barbarian Axe	1"	2	4+	4+	-	1
Barbarian Flail	2"	1	4+	3+	-	1

DESCRIPTION

A unit of Chaos Marauders has any number of models, each armed with one of the following weapon options: Barbarian Axe and Darkwood Shield; or Barbarian Flail.

MARAUDER CHIEFTAIN: 1 model in this unit can be a Marauder Chieftain. Add 1 to the Attacks characteristic of that model's melee weapons.

ICON BEARER: 1 in every 5 models in this unit can be an Icon Bearer. Subtract 1 from the Bravery characteristic of enemy units while they are within 6" of any friendly Icon Bearers.

BARBARIAN DRUMMER: 1 in every 5 models in this unit can be a Barbarian Drummer. Add 1 to run and charge rolls for this unit while it includes any Barbarian Drummers.

MARK OF CHAOS: When you select this unit to be part of your army, you must give it one of the following Mark of Chaos keywords: **Khorne, Tzeentch, Nurgle, Slaanesh** or **Undivided**.

ABILITIES

Barbarian Hordes: *When a Marauder horde masses, entire enemy regiments can be swept away under a tide of barbarous muscle.*

Add 1 to hit rolls for attacks made by this unit while it has at least 10 models. In addition, improve the Rend characteristic of this unit's melee weapons by 1 while it has at least 20 models.

Boundless Ferocity: *When the barbarous worshippers of Chaos smell death in the air, it is almost impossible to restrain their furious battle-lust.*

When you make a charge roll for this unit, change the lowest dice in that roll to a 6. If the roll is a double, change one of the dice to a 6 instead.

Darkwood Shields: *Though crude in appearance, these shields are still capable of providing a measure of defence against all but the most determined attacks.*

Add 1 to save rolls for attacks that target a unit with Darkwood Shields.

KEYWORDS	CHAOS, MORTAL, SLAVES TO DARKNESS, MARK OF CHAOS, CHAOS MARAUDERS

MOVE 12"
WOUNDS 2
SAVE 6+
BRAVERY 5

CHAOS MARAUDER HORSEMEN

Riding at the vanguard of the Chaos hosts come the Marauder Horsemen. These skilled mounted warriors launch daring raids on the enemy lines before pulling back, luring the foe closer before turning around and hacking them to pieces.

MISSILE WEAPONS	Range	Attacks	To Hit	To Wound	Rend	Damage
Marauder Javelin	12"	1	4+	3+	-1	1
MELEE WEAPONS	**Range**	**Attacks**	**To Hit**	**To Wound**	**Rend**	**Damage**
Barbarian Axe	1"	2	4+	4+	-	1
Marauder Javelin	2"	1	4+	3+	-	1
Barbarian Flail	2"	1	4+	3+	-1	1
Trampling Hooves	1"	2	4+	4+	-	1

DESCRIPTION

A unit of Chaos Marauder Horsemen has any number of models, each armed with one of the following weapon options: Barbarian Axe and Darkwood Shield; Marauder Javelin and Darkwood Shield; or Barbarian Flail.

MOUNT: This unit's Chaos Steeds attack with their Trampling Hooves.

HORSEMASTER: 1 model in this unit can be a Horsemaster. Add 1 to the Attacks characteristic of a Horsemaster's melee weapons.

ICON BEARER: 1 in every 5 models in this unit can be an Icon Bearer. Subtract 1 from the Bravery characteristic of enemy units while they are within 6" of any friendly Icon Bearers.

HORNBLOWER: 1 in every 5 models in this unit can be a Hornblower. Add 1 to run and charge rolls for this unit while it includes any Hornblowers.

MARK OF CHAOS: When you select this unit to be part of your army, you must give it one of the following Mark of Chaos keywords: Khorne, Tzeentch, Nurgle, Slaanesh or Undivided.

ABILITIES

Barbarian Hordes: *When a Marauder horde masses, entire enemy regiments can be swept away under a tide of barbarous muscle.*

Add 1 to hit rolls for attacks made by this unit while it has at least 10 models.

Darkwood Shields: *Though crude in appearance, these shields are still capable of providing a measure of defence against all but the most determined attacks.*

Add 1 to save rolls for attacks that target a unit with Darkwood Shields.

Feigned Flight: *Marauder Horsemen are talented raiders, and have great skill in the art of hit-and-run attacks.*

This unit can retreat and still shoot and/or charge later in the same turn.

KEYWORDS	CHAOS, MORTAL, SLAVES TO DARKNESS, MARK OF CHAOS, CHAOS MARAUDER HORSEMEN

SOUL GRINDER

108

MOVE 16

SAVE 4+

WOUNDS 10

BRAVERY

There is no act of destruction a Soul Grinder will not commit in an effort to complete the tithe of death demanded from it. These clanking daemon engines scuttle forth on huge mechanical legs, unable to rest while a single foe draws breath.

MISSILE WEAPONS	Range	Attacks	To Hit	To Wound	Rend	Damage
Harvester Cannon	16"	✹	4+	3+	-1	1
Phlegm Bombardment	20"	1	4+	3+	-2	3
MELEE WEAPONS	**Range**	**Attacks**	**To Hit**	**To Wound**	**Rend**	**Damage**
Piston-driven Legs	1"	✹	4+	3+	-1	1
Hellforged Claw	2"	1	4+	3+	-2	D6
Warpmetal Blade	2"	2	4+	3+	-2	3
Daemonbone Talon	2"	4	3+	3+	-1	D3

DAMAGE TABLE			
Wounds Suffered	Move	Harvester Cannon	Piston-driven Legs
0-3	12"	6	6
4-6	10"	5	5
7-10	8"	4	4
11-13	7"	3	3
14+	6"	2	2

DESCRIPTION

A Soul Grinder is a single model armed with a Harvester Cannon, Phlegm Bombardment, Hellforged Claw, Piston-driven Legs and one of the following weapon options: Warpmetal Blade; or Daemonbone Talon.

MARK OF CHAOS: When you select this model to be part of your army, you must give it one of the following Mark of Chaos keywords: **Khorne, Tzeentch, Nurgle, Slaanesh** or **Undivided**.

ABILITIES

Hellforged Claw: *The crushing force of a Hellforged Claw can obliterate anything unfortunate enough to be caught in its grasp.*

If the unmodified hit roll for an attack made with a Hellforged Claw is 6, that attack inflicts D6 mortal wounds on the target and the attack sequence ends (do not make a wound or save roll).

Implacable Advance: *This daemonic engine is utterly relentless in its desire to pay off the soul-tithe owed to its masters.*

This model can run and still shoot later in the same turn.

KEYWORDS	CHAOS, DAEMON, SLAVES TO DARKNESS, MONSTER, MARK OF CHAOS, SOUL GRINDER

SLAUGHTERBRUTE

MOVE

WOUNDS 12 **SAVE** 4+

7

BRAVERY

Even the greatest champions cannot hope to bind a Slaughterbrute through physical might alone. Only through specially forged blades of binding can these monstrosities be controlled, and their boundless fury directed towards their master's enemies.

MELEE WEAPONS	Range	Attacks	To Hit	To Wound	Rend	Damage
Razor-tipped Claws	2"	☀	4+	3+	-1	D3
Mighty Jaws	1"	2	4+	☀	-	3
Slashing Talons	1"	2	4+	3+	-	1

DAMAGE TABLE			
Wounds Suffered	Move	Razor-tipped Claws	Mighty Jaws
0-2	10"	6	1+
3-4	8"	5	2+
5-7	8"	4	3+
8-9	6"	3	4+
10+	4"	2	5+

DESCRIPTION

A Slaughterbrute is a single model armed with Razor-tipped Claws, Mighty Jaws and Slashing Talons.

MARK OF CHAOS: When you select this model to be part of your army, you can give it the following Mark of Chaos keyword: KHORNE.

ABILITIES

Sigils of Enslavement: *By carving runes of domination into a Slaughterbrute's back and driving cursed blades of binding into its flesh, the monster's will can be bound to a Champion of Chaos.*

When this model is set up for the first time, you can pick 1 friendly SLAVES TO DARKNESS HERO on the battlefield to be its master. Add 1 to hit rolls for attacks made by this model while it is wholly within 12" of that HERO. The same HERO cannot be the master of more than 1 SLAUGHTERBRUTE.

Beast Unbound: *A masterless Slaughterbrute is a terrifying force of destruction, running rampant and attacking anything that comes near.*

If this model is within 6" of an enemy unit and more than 12" from its master (see left) at the start of the charge phase, you must roll a dice. On a 4+, the closest other unit within 6" of this model immediately suffers D3 mortal wounds.

KEYWORDS	CHAOS, MONSTER, SLAVES TO DARKNESS, SLAUGHTERBRUTE

MUTALITH VORTEX BEAST

MOVE	*
WOUNDS	12
SAVE	4+
BRAVERY	7

Within the pulsating star suspended above the back of a Mutalith Vortex Beast can be found a portal to the Realm of Chaos itself. These horrific monsters constantly seethe with the power of mutation, those around them rewrought into horrific forms.

MELEE WEAPONS	Range	Attacks	To Hit	To Wound	Rend	Damage
Crushing Claws	2"	4	4+	*	-1	D3
Betentacled Maw	2"	*	4+	4+	-	1

DAMAGE TABLE			
Wounds Suffered	Move	Crushing Claws	Betentacled Maw
0-2	10"	1+	3D6
3-4	8"	2+	2D6
5-7	8"	3+	D6
8-9	6"	4+	D3
10+	4"	5+	1

DESCRIPTION

A Mutalith Vortex Beast is a single model armed with Crushing Claws and a Betentacled Maw.

MARK OF CHAOS: When you select this model to be part of your army, you can give it the following Mark of Chaos keyword: TZEENTCH.

ABILITIES

Mutant Regeneration: *This unnatural abomination is invigorated by the raw power of Chaos.*

In your hero phase, you can heal up to D3 wounds allocated to this model.

Aura of Mutation: *Merely standing in the presence of a Mutalith can have horrific consequences.*

In your hero phase, you can pick 1 enemy unit within 18" of this model, roll a dice and look up the effect on the table below:

D6	Effect
1	**Hideous Disfigurement:** *The faces of the enemy are disfigured by the mutating touch of Chaos.* Subtract 1 from the Bravery characteristic of the unit for the rest of the battle.
2	**Troggbrains:** *Waves of Chaos energy assail the enemy, striking them dumb and making them stagger about blindly.* Subtract 1 from run rolls made for the unit for the rest of the battle.
3	**Gift of Mutations:** *The legs of the enemy are mutated into twisted, limping parodies of their previous forms.* Subtract 1" from the Move characteristic of the unit for the rest of the battle.
4	**Tide of Transmogrification:** *Horror spreads through the enemy ranks as their bodies turn messily inside out.* The unit suffers D3 mortal wounds.
5	**Maelstrom of Change:** *Nearby opponents are reduced to madness as their minds are blasted by the glory of Chaos.* The unit suffers D6 mortal wounds.
6	**Spawnchange:** *Groups of enemies are lost in the blink of an eye as they are broken and twisted into new and hideous forms.* The unit suffers D6 mortal wounds. If any models from the unit are slain by these mortal wounds, you can set up 1 SLAVES TO DARKNESS CHAOS SPAWN with the same Mark of Chaos keyword as this model within 3" of the unit (or, if the unit was destroyed, the last model from the unit to be slain) and add it to your army. If you do not add a SLAVES TO DARKNESS CHAOS SPAWN to your army, you can heal up to D3 wounds allocated to this model.

KEYWORDS	CHAOS, SLAVES TO DARKNESS, MONSTER, MUTALITH VORTEX BEAST

FURIES

MOVE	12"
WOUNDS	2
SAVE	-
BRAVERY	10

Furies are spiteful daemonic imps that throng those lands under the sway of Chaos. Though individually weak, when they swarm they can prove surprisingly deadly, waiting until the foe's back is turned before launching vicious hit-and-run attacks.

MELEE WEAPONS	Range	Attacks	To Hit	To Wound	Rend	Damage
Razor-sharp Dagger and Claws	1"	2	4+	3+	-1	1

DESCRIPTION

A unit of Furies has any number of models, each armed with a Razor-sharp Dagger and Claws.

FLY: This unit can fly.

ABILITIES

Sneaky Little Devils: *Furies are spiteful creatures that utterly loathe the idea of engaging in a fair fight, much preferring – where possible – to stab distracted enemies in the back.*

In the combat phase, when you pick this unit to fight, you can say it will cower instead of fighting. If you do so, this unit must make a normal move and must retreat.

KEYWORDS	CHAOS, DAEMON, SLAVES TO DARKNESS, FURIES

RAPTORYX

MOVE	10"
WOUNDS	2
SAVE	-
BRAVERY	6

One of the many forms of wildlife twisted by the power of Chaos, Raptoryx cross the land in vast flocks. Cunning and vicious beasts, they are willing to take on prey many times their size, pulling them down in a frenzy of slashing talons and snapping beaks.

MELEE WEAPONS	Range	Attacks	To Hit	To Wound	Rend	Damage
Razor-sharp Beak and Talons	1"	2	3+	3+	-	1

DESCRIPTION

A unit of Raptoryx has any number of models, each armed with a Razor-sharp Beak and Talons.

ABILITIES

Crazed Flock: *A flock of snapping, screeching Raptoryx is capable of swiftly bringing down any prey should they catch them unawares.*

Add 1 to the Attacks characteristic of this unit's melee weapons if it made a charge move in the same turn.

KEYWORDS	CHAOS, SLAVES TO DARKNESS, RAPTORYX

● WARSCROLL ●

SPLINTERED FANG

MOVE	6"
WOUNDS	1
SAVE	5+
BRAVERY	5

The mystic leaders of the Splintered Fang lead their people in worship of the Coiling Ones, serpentine daemons who embody cunning and might. Poison is the greatest weapon of the Fangs, and a single cut from their blades can prove fatal.

MELEE WEAPONS	Range	Attacks	To Hit	To Wound	Rend	Damage
Poisoned Weapons	1"	1	4+	4+	-	1

DESCRIPTION

A unit of Splintered Fang has any number of models, each armed with Poisoned Weapons.

TRUEBLOOD: 1 in every 10 models in this unit must be a Trueblood. Add 1 to the Attacks characteristic of a Trueblood's melee weapons.

SERPENT CALLER: 1 in every 10 models in this unit must be a Serpent Caller.

SERPENTS: 1 in every 10 models in this unit must be a Serpents model. Serpents models have a Wounds characteristic of 2.

ABILITIES

One Cut, One Kill: *The warriors of the Splintered Fang coat their blades with vile poisons before every battle.*

If the unmodified hit roll for an attack made by this unit is 6, that attack inflicts 1 mortal wound on the target and the attack sequence ends (do not make a wound or save roll).

Snake Charmer: *Serpent Callers can summon their slithering familiars as if from nowhere.*

You can return 1 slain Serpents model to this unit in your hero phase if this unit includes any Serpent Callers. Set up the returning model within 1" of a model from this unit. The returning model can only be set up within 3" of an enemy unit if any models from this unit are already within 3" of that enemy unit.

KEYWORDS	CHAOS, MORTAL, SLAVES TO DARKNESS, CULTISTS, SPLINTERED FANG

● WARSCROLL ●

CORVUS CABAL

MOVE	8"
WOUNDS	1
SAVE	6+
BRAVERY	5

Agile and avaricious, the murder-cultists of the Corvus Cabal descend on their prey from above. Always hunting for worthy trinkets to offer the Great Gatherer, chaotic patron of cut-throats and thieves, the Cabal strike without warning or mercy.

MISSILE WEAPONS	Range	Attacks	To Hit	To Wound	Rend	Damage
Raven Darts	8"	1	4+	5+	-	1

MELEE WEAPONS	Range	Attacks	To Hit	To Wound	Rend	Damage
Corvus Weapons	1"	1	4+	4+	-	1

DESCRIPTION

A unit of Corvus Cabal has any number of models, each armed with Corvus Weapons and Raven Darts.

SHADOW PIERCER: 1 in every 9 models in this unit must be a Shadow Piercer. Add 1 to the Attacks characteristic of a Shadow Piercer's melee weapons.

SHRIKE TALON: 1 in every 9 models in this unit must be a Shrike Talon. You can re-roll 1s in charge rolls made for this unit while it includes any Shrike Talons.

ABILITIES

Death From Above: *The Corvus Cabal favour stalking their prey and striking from unexpected angles.*

When this unit makes a move, it can pass across terrain features in the same manner as a model that can fly.

KEYWORDS	CHAOS, MORTAL, SLAVES TO DARKNESS, CULTISTS, CORVUS CABAL

• WARSCROLL •

THE UNMADE

The island of Tzlid, drifting ever closer to the Shyish Nadir, is home to the cannibal
tribes of the Unmade. The self-mutilation performed by these pain worshippers is
horrifying to behold, and their leaders are visions from the darkest of nightmares.

MELEE WEAPONS	Range	Attacks	To Hit	To Wound	Rend	Damage
Maiming Weapons	1"	1	4+	4+	-	1
Nightmare Sickles	1"	3	4+	3+	-1	2

DESCRIPTION

A unit of Unmade has any number of models,
each armed with Maiming Weapons.

BLISSFUL ONE: 1 in every 9 models in this
unit must be a Blissful One. A Blissful One
is armed with Nightmare Sickles instead of
Maiming Weapons.

JOYOUS ONE: 1 in every 9 models in this unit
must be a Joyous One. Add 1 to the Attacks
characteristic of a Joyous One's melee weapons.

ABILITIES

Frozen in Fear: *The self-inflicted mutilation
performed by the Unmade is a sight disturbing
enough to momentarily freeze even a veteran
warrior in horror.*

Subtract 1 from the Bravery characteristic of
enemy units while they are within 6" of any
friendly units with this ability. In addition,
enemy units within 3" of this unit cannot retreat.

KEYWORDS	CHAOS, MORTAL, SLAVES TO DARKNESS, CULTISTS, UNMADE

• WARSCROLL •

CYPHER LORDS

The Cypher Lords seek not only to defeat their foes, but to drive them to insanity, for
they believe madness is the purest form of Chaos. In battle, the alchemical bombs and
illusory tactics of these Hyshian cultists render them almost impossible to pin down.

MISSILE WEAPONS	Range	Attacks	To Hit	To Wound	Rend	Damage
Throwing Stars and Chakrams	8"	1	4+	5+	-	1
MELEE WEAPONS	**Range**	**Attacks**	**To Hit**	**To Wound**	**Rend**	**Damage**
Exotic Blades	1"	1	4+	4+	-	1

DESCRIPTION

A unit of Cypher Lords has any number of
models, each armed with Exotic Blades and
Throwing Stars and Chakrams.

THRALLMASTER: 1 in every 8 models in this
unit must be a Thrallmaster.

LUMINATE: 1 in every 8 models in this
unit must be a Luminate. Add 1 to charge rolls for
this unit while it includes any Luminates.

ABILITIES

Shattered Gloom Globe: *Thrallmasters carry
globes that release dense clouds of shimmersmoke
when shattered, choking the foe and masking the
Cypher Lords' advance.*

While this unit includes any Thrallmasters,
at the start of the combat phase you can pick
1 enemy unit within 3" of this unit and roll a
dice. On a 4+, subtract 1 from hit rolls for that
unit until your next hero phase. The same unit
cannot be affected by this ability more than once
per turn.

KEYWORDS	CHAOS, MORTAL, SLAVES TO DARKNESS, CULTISTS, CYPHER LORDS

SPIRE TYRANTS

MOVE	6"
WOUNDS	1
SAVE	5+
BRAVERY	5

Each member of the Spire Tyrants has earned glory and renown in the fighting pits of the Varanspire. These ferocious gladiators constantly seek new and deadlier challenges, believing themselves to be favoured by Archaon himself.

MELEE WEAPONS	Range	Attacks	To Hit	To Wound	Rend	Damage
Gladiatorial Weapons	1"	1	4+	4+	-	1

DESCRIPTION

A unit of Spire Tyrants has any number of models, each armed with Gladiatorial Weapons.

PIT CHAMPION: 1 in every 9 models in this unit must be a Pit Champion. Add 2 to the Attacks characteristic of a Pit Champion's melee weapons.

HEADCLAIMER: 1 in every 9 models in this unit must be a Headclaimer. Add 1 to the Damage characteristic of a Headclaimer's melee weapons.

BESTIGOR DESTROYER: 1 in every 9 models in this unit must be a Bestigor Destroyer. Add 2 to the Attacks characteristic of a Bestigor Destroyer's melee weapons.

ABILITIES

Pit Fighters: *Years of experience in the Varanspire's fighting pits have made the Spire Tyrants into brutally efficient killers.*

You can add 1 to hit rolls for attacks made by this unit if it charged in the same turn.

KEYWORDS | CHAOS, MORTAL, SLAVES TO DARKNESS, CULTISTS, SPIRE TYRANTS

IRON GOLEMS

Skilled blacksmiths, the Iron Golems believe themselves chosen to provide arms and armour to Archaon's forces. Amongst the war-wracked lands of Chamon, their legions are renowned for their dauntless resilience and chilling efficiency.

MOVE **5"**
WOUNDS **1**
SAVE **4+**
BRAVERY **6**

MISSILE WEAPONS	Range	Attacks	To Hit	To Wound	Rend	Damage
Bolas	8"	1	4+	4+	-	1
MELEE WEAPONS	Range	Attacks	To Hit	To Wound	Rend	Damage
Legion Weapons	1"	1	4+	4+	-	1

DESCRIPTION

A unit of Iron Golems has any number of models, each armed with Legion Weapons and Bolas.

DOMINAR: 1 in every 8 models in this unit must be a Dominar. Add 1 to the Attacks characteristic of a Dominar's melee weapons.

SIGNIFER: 1 in every 8 models in this unit must be a Signifer. Add 2 to the Bravery characteristic of this unit while it includes any Signifers.

OGOR BREACHER: 1 in every 8 models in this unit must be an Ogor Breacher. Ogor Breachers have a Wounds characteristic of 3.

ABILITIES

Iron Resilience: *At a barked command from their Dominar, the legionaries of the Iron Golems snap into an impenetrable shieldwall.*

You can re-roll save rolls for attacks that target this unit if this unit has not made a normal move in the same turn.

KEYWORDS	CHAOS, MORTAL, SLAVES TO DARKNESS, CULTISTS, IRON GOLEMS

UNTAMED BEASTS

By devouring the flesh of Ghur's many predators, the Untamed Beasts seek to gain their strength and power. These shamanistic savages worship Chaos as the Devourer of Existence, and are peerless trackers and hunters.

MOVE **6"**
WOUNDS **1**
SAVE **6+**
BRAVERY **5**

MISSILE WEAPONS	Range	Attacks	To Hit	To Wound	Rend	Damage
Jagged Harpoon	8"	1	4+	3+	-1	2
MELEE WEAPONS	Range	Attacks	To Hit	To Wound	Rend	Damage
Hunting Weapons	1"	1	4+	4+	-	1

DESCRIPTION

A unit of Untamed Beasts has any number of models, each armed with Hunting Weapons.

HEART-EATER: 1 in every 9 models in this unit must be a Heart-eater. Add 1 to the Attacks characteristic of a Heart-eater's melee weapons.

FIRST FANG: 1 in every 9 models in this unit must be a First Fang. A First Fang is armed with a Jagged Harpoon in addition to their other weapons.

ROCKTUSK PROWLER: 1 in every 9 models in this unit must be a Rocktusk Prowler. Rocktusk Prowlers have a Wounds characteristic of 2.

ABILITIES

Unleash the Beast: *With bursts of primal energy, the Untamed Beasts chase down their enemies with relentless fervour.*

This unit can run and still charge later in the same turn. In addition, after armies are set up but before the first battle round begins, this unit can move up to 6".

KEYWORDS	CHAOS, MORTAL, SLAVES TO DARKNESS, CULTISTS, UNTAMED BEASTS

MINDSTEALER SPHIRANX

116 | MOVE **10"** | WOUNDS **10** | SAVE **5+** | BRAVERY **10**

Mindstealer Sphiranxes are powerful and sinister telepaths. These cruel-hearted beasts enjoy nothing more than toying with their prey, plundering their innermost secrets before summarily ripping them to shreds with sharpened claws.

MELEE WEAPONS	Range	Attacks	To Hit	To Wound	Rend	Damage
Shredding Claws	1"	3	3+	3+	-1	1
Lashing Tail	1"	2	4+	3+	-	1

DESCRIPTION

A Mindstealer Sphiranx is a single model armed with Shredding Claws and a Lashing Tail.

ABILITIES

Telepathic Dread: *A Mindstealer Sphiranx delights in casting themself into the minds of their prey, and assailing them with visions of their deepest fears.*

Subtract 2 from the Bravery characteristic of enemy units while they are within 12" of any friendly models with this ability.

Dominate Mind: *A Sphiranx can manipulate the actions of their enemies with a simple glance.*

In your hero phase, you can pick 1 enemy unit within 12" of this model that is visible to it. If

you do so, both you and your opponent must secretly place a dice so that it shows any number, then reveal them. If the numbers shown on the dice are the same, this ability has no effect. If the numbers shown on the dice are different, the enemy unit you picked fights at the end of the combat phase until the next battle round. You cannot pick the same unit as the target for this ability more than once in the same turn (whether this ability has an effect or not).

KEYWORDS	CHAOS, MORTAL, MONSTER, SLAVES TO DARKNESS, MINDSTEALER SPHIRANX

FOMOROID CRUSHER

| MOVE **6"** | WOUNDS **10** | SAVE **5+** | BRAVERY **10**

Brutish creatures from a lost age, the Fomoroid Crushers now exist only to tear down and destroy. In battle they fly into a terrible rage, torturous memories of the creatures they once were lending their blows a maddened strength.

MISSILE WEAPONS	Range	Attacks	To Hit	To Wound	Rend	Damage
Hurled Terrain	12"	2	3+	3+	-1	2
MELEE WEAPONS	**Range**	**Attacks**	**To Hit**	**To Wound**	**Rend**	**Damage**
Crushing Fists	1"	4	3+	3+	-	2

DESCRIPTION

A Fomoroid Crusher is a single model armed with Crushing Fists and Hurled Terrain.

ABILITIES

Rampage: *When this hulking beast strides into combat, the doom of its enemies is all but assured.*

After this model makes a charge move, you can pick 1 enemy unit within 1" of this model and roll a number of dice equal to the charge roll for that charge move. For each 6, that unit suffers 1 mortal wound.

Insurmountable Strength: *The raw might of a Fomoroid Crusher sees them use the very environment as a weapon, swinging chunks of broken masonry or uprooted trees to crush the life from any who get in their way.*

In your hero phase, pick 1 terrain feature within 6" of this model and roll a dice for each other unit within 6" of that terrain feature. On a 3+, that unit suffers D3 mortal wounds.

KEYWORDS	CHAOS, MORTAL, MONSTER, SLAVES TO DARKNESS, FOMOROID CRUSHER

• ENDLESS SPELL WARSCROLL •

EIGHTFOLD DOOM-SIGIL

Eightfold Doom-Sigils are icons of Chaos in all its glory, blazing symbols of pure ruin. To fall in the presence of such a sorcerous construct is to be damned, for these lingering spells hungrily suck souls into the Realm of Chaos for the gods to feast upon, and a measure of this siphoned power is offered to those devoted who fight in the icon's shadow.

DESCRIPTION

An Eightfold Doom-Sigil is a single model.

MAGIC

Summon Eightfold Doom-Sigil: *Chanting invocations to the all-encompassing essence of undivided ruin, the shaman summons a burning icon of Chaotic supremacy.*

Summon Eightfold Doom-Sigil has a casting value of 5. Only **Slaves to Darkness Wizards** can attempt to cast this spell. If successfully cast, set up an Eightfold Doom-Sigil model wholly within 12" of the caster.

ABILITIES

Empowered by Atrocity: *The souls of those slain in the presence of an Eightfold Doom-Sigil are absorbed by the magical manifestation, feeding the Dark Gods' eternal hunger and inspiring those mortal servants who fight nearby to battle on – even as their own lives are offered in tribute.*

Keep track of the number of models that are slain within 12" of this model each turn. At the end of each turn, roll a dice for each model that was slain within 12" of this model during that turn. For each 3+, the player whose turn is taking place must pick 1 **Slaves to Darkness** unit wholly within 18" of this model. Add 1 to the Attacks characteristic of that unit's melee weapons (excluding those of mounts) until that player's next hero phase. A unit cannot benefit from this ability more than once per turn.

KEYWORDS	ENDLESS SPELL, EIGHTFOLD DOOM-SIGIL

• ENDLESS SPELL WARSCROLL •

DARKFIRE DAEMONRIFT

Darkfire Daemonrifts are eldritch portals torn ajar by the darkest of incantations. Once the veil has been sundered the raw magic seeping from the Realm of Chaos forms an opening for the horrors beyond to vent their spite, widened and empowered further by spellcraft that draws upon the essence of Chaos.

DESCRIPTION

A Darkfire Daemonrift is a single model.

PREDATORY: A Darkfire Daemonrift is a predatory endless spell. It can move up to 12" and can fly.

MAGIC

Summon Darkfire Daemonrift: *Reciting the names of ancient daemonic entities in the Dark Tongue, the sorcerer focuses their will to wrench the veil between the realms and the essence of Chaos wide open.*

Summon Darkfire Daemonrift has a casting value of 6. Only **Slaves to Darkness Wizards** can attempt to cast this spell. If successfully cast, set up a Darkfire Daemonrift model wholly within 9" of the caster.

ABILITIES

Reality Screams: *Once the skin of reality has been breached it is difficult to close, and so Darkfire Daemonrifts seem to move at random – the crack 'healing' in one place only to suddenly reappear and vent a gout of mutative witchflame elsewhere.*

When this model is set up, the player who set it up can immediately make a move with it.

Billowing Energies: *From the maw of a Darkfire Daemonrift foul predators from beyond unleash streams of Chaotic energy on their hapless victims.*

After this model has moved, each unit that has any models it passed across, and each other unit that is within 1" of it at the end of its move, suffers D3 mortal wounds.

Fuelled by Sorcery: *A Darkfire Daemonrift absorbs magical power, widening further and expelling more powerful gouts of ruinous energy as it hungrily devours arcane energies.*

Add 1 to the number of mortal wounds inflicted by this endless spell for each **Wizard** and each other **Endless Spell** within 12" of this model after it has moved.

KEYWORDS	ENDLESS SPELL, DARKFIRE DAEMONRIFT

REALMSCOURGE RUPTURE

Even by the standards of Chaos sorceries, Realmscourge Ruptures are not subtle weapons. When the necessary magical power has been channelled and released by a tribal shaman, the land itself writhes in the grip of Chaos, sharpened spikes surging forth like an accursed tidal wave to overwhelm anything in their path.

DESCRIPTION

A Realmscourge Rupture is a single model.

PREDATORY: A Realmscourge Rupture is a predatory endless spell. It can move up to 9" and can fly.

MAGIC

Summon Realmscourge Rupture: *Slamming their staff against the earth, the sorcerer calls forth the power of a Realmscourge Rupture.*

Summon Realmscourge Rupture has a casting value of 7. Only **Slaves to Darkness Wizards** can attempt to cast this spell. If successfully cast, set up a Realmscourge Rupture model wholly within 9" of the caster.

ABILITIES

Oncoming Annihilation: *Once a Realmscourge Rupture has been conjured and let loose, it is almost impossible to stop.*

When this model is set up, the player who set it up can immediately make a move with it.

Tide of Ruin: *Realmscourge Ruptures surge across the battlefield as an inevitable wave of death, their jagged spikes retracting into the earth only to erupt once more further along the path of destruction.*

Whenever you set up a Realmscourge Rupture, you must place it widthways in the direction you wish it to move. Whenever it moves, move it in a straight line in that direction (it cannot move backwards).

Debilitating Shockwave: *The vicious spikes that erupt from an onrushing Realmscourge Rupture not only impale any unfortunate enough to be struck by them, but also send those nearby staggering through the tremors that rock the tortured earth.*

After this model has moved, each unit that has any models it passed across, and each other unit that is within 1" of it at the end of its move, suffers D3 mortal wounds.

In addition, until the end of the battle round, halve the Move characteristic of each unit that has any models it passed across, and each other unit that is within 1" of it at the end of its move.

KEYWORDS	ENDLESS SPELL, REALMSCOURGE RUPTURE

The magic of the Dark Gods floods the battlefield with malefic energy, twisting the realms into an image more pleasing to the Ruinous Powers.

PITCHED BATTLE PROFILES

The table below provides points, minimum and maximum unit sizes, and battlefield roles for the warscrolls and warscroll battalions in this book, for use in Pitched Battles. Spending the points listed on this table allows you to take a minimum-sized unit with any of its upgrades. Understrength units cost the full amount of points. Larger units are taken in multiples of their minimum unit size; multiply their cost by the same amount as you multiplied their size. If a unit has two points values separated by a slash (e.g. '60/200'), the second value is for a maximum sized unit. Units that are listed as 'Unique' are named characters and can only be taken once in an army. A unit that has any of the keywords listed on the Allies table can be taken as an allied unit by a Slaves to Darkness army. Updated December 2019; the profiles printed here take precedence over any profiles with an earlier publication date or no publication date.

SLAVES TO DARKNESS WARSCROLL	UNIT SIZE MIN	UNIT SIZE MAX	POINTS	BATTLEFIELD ROLE	NOTES
Chaos Marauders	20	40	150	Battleline	
Chaos Warriors	5	30	100	Battleline	
Chaos Warshrine	1	1	170	Behemoth	
Mutalith Vortex Beast	1	1	170	Behemoth	
Slaughterbrute	1	1	170	Behemoth	
Soul Grinder	1	1	210	Behemoth	
Archaon the Everchosen	1	1	800	Leader, Behemoth	Unique
Chaos Lord on Manticore	1	1	280	Leader, Behemoth	
Chaos Sorcerer Lord on Manticore	1	1	260	Leader, Behemoth	
Be'lakor	1	1	240	Leader	Unique
Chaos Lord	1	1	110	Leader	
Chaos Lord on Daemonic Mount	1	1	170	Leader	
Chaos Lord on Karkadrak	1	1	250	Leader	
Chaos Sorcerer Lord	1	1	110	Leader	
Slaves to Darkness Daemon Prince	1	1	210	Leader	
Darkoath Chieftain	1	1	90	Leader	
Darkoath Warqueen	1	1	90	Leader	
Exalted Hero of Chaos	1	1	90	Leader	
Gaunt Summoner on Disc of Tzeentch	1	1	260	Leader	
Ogroid Myrmidon	1	1	140	Leader	
Theddra Skull-Scryer	1	1	70	Leader	Unique. These units must be taken as a set for a total of 130 points. Although taken as a set, each is a separate unit.
Godsworn Hunt	5	5	60		
Chaos Chariots	1	3	120		Battleline in Slaves to Darkness army
Chaos Chosen	5	20	140		
Chaos Knights	5	20	180		Battleline in Slaves to Darkness army
Chaos Marauder Horsemen	5	30	90		Battleline in Slaves to Darkness army
Corvus Cabal	9	36	70		
Cypher Lords	8	32	70		
Slaves to Darkness Chaos Spawn	1	6	50		
Fomoroid Crusher	1	1	100		
Furies	6	30	100		
Gorebeast Chariots	1	3	150		
Iron Golems	8	32	70		
Mindstealer Sphiranx	1	1	100		
Raptoryx	6	30	90		
Spire Tyrants	9	36	70		
Splintered Fang	10	40	70		
The Unmade	9	36	70		
Untamed Beasts	9	36	70		

SLAVES TO DARKNESS WARSCROLL	UNIT SIZE MIN	MAX	POINTS	BATTLEFIELD ROLE	NOTES
Varanguard	3	12	300		Battleline in Slaves to Darkness army if all units are HOST OF THE EVERCHOSEN
Bloodmarked Warband	-	-	180	*Warscroll Battalion*	
Chaos Horde	-	-	140	*Warscroll Battalion*	
Fatesworn Warband	-	-	180	*Warscroll Battalion*	
Godsworn Champions of Ruin	-	-	180	*Warscroll Battalion*	
Godswrath Warband	-	-	180	*Warscroll Battalion*	
Overlords of Chaos	-	-	120	*Warscroll Battalion*	
Plaguetouched Warband	-	-	180	*Warscroll Battalion*	
Pleasurebound Warband	-	-	160	*Warscroll Battalion*	
Ruinbringer Warband	-	-	140	*Warscroll Battalion*	
Eightfold Doom-Sigil	1	1	40	*Endless Spell*	
Darkfire Daemonrift	1	1	50	*Endless Spell*	
Realmscourge Rupture	1	1	60	*Endless Spell*	

FACTION	ALLIES
Slaves to Darkness	Beasts of Chaos, Khorne, Tzeentch, Nurgle, Slaanesh